Welcome

Congratulations: picking up this book is the first step towards what could be a life-changing experience. I've built and run a number of businesses in the past ten years, and have had my share of failures as well as successes. This book distils what I've learned in that time, along with the best practice of some of the industry's leaders.

The aim of this book is to set you on the right path towards running your own successful online business. It covers three essential areas: coming up with the right product; building a platform to sell that product; and connecting with the right customers.

You don't need to be an IT expert to launch an online business, and this book reflects that. What you do need is imagination, open-mindedness and determination.

Nor is this a "get rich quick" book. It's a realistic guide to setting up in business, and pulls no punches about the hard work and stamina that are needed to make a success.

The good news is that it's possible to set up an online business on a low budget. You don't need premises or high levels of stock. It also opens up a potentially huge audience to sell to, and you can be up and running much more quickly than a traditional business. You can see this in practice: in tandem with the writing of this book, I built a real, working business at www.makingyourowncandles.co.uk

Plan it, build it and sell it: get those three steps right and you have every chance of making a success of your bright idea.

Best of luck!

Kevin Partner is creator and owner of NlightN Multimedia Ltd (www.nlightn.co.uk), Scribbleit Ltd (www.scribbleit.co.uk) and PassYourTheory Ltd (www.passyourtheory.co.uk).

NlightN was founded in 1999 and provides e-learning and web application development to corporate clients. Its latest product is www.greetingcardmaker.co.uk, a greetings card creation service.

Scribbleit was created in 2003 and provides writing and programming to large and small businesses. PassYourTheory.co.uk was launched in 2005 and is the UK's leading driving theory test training service.

Kevin has been a Contributing Editor to PC Pro since 1996, writing on multimedia and web applications.

Follow Kevin on Twitter (www.twitter.com/kevpartner), on his blog at www.scribbleit.co.uk and in the PC Pro blogs at www.pcpro.co.uk/blogs/author/kevin-partner

Contents

Planning
Start the right business

Skills

PHYSICAL
- ☐ Stamina
- ☐ Agility
- ☐ Fitness
- ☐ Building things
- ☐ Cooking
- ☐ Using machines and tools
- ☐ Gardening

RTS
- Creativity
- Design
- nagination

- ☐ Performance arts
- ☐ Improvisation
- ☐ Visual arts
- ☐ Crafts

- ☐ Teaching
- ☐ Coaching
- ☐ Leading
- ☐ Managing others
- ☐ Self-management
- ☐ Decisiveness

Results are tailored to English, United Kingdom Edit

How would you like to generate keyword ideas? | Enter one keyw
- ◉ Descriptive words or phrases (e.g. green tea) | candle making / candle making
- ○ Website content (e.g. www.example.co.uk/product?id=74893) | ☑ Use synony
▸ Filter my resu
Get keyword i

Choose columns to be displayed: ⓘ
Show/hide columns ▾

Keywords	Advertiser Competition ⓘ	▼ Local Search Volume: May ⓘ
Keywords related to term(s) entered - sort by relevance ⓘ		
candle making		
candle making kit		74,000
making candles		8,100
make candle		3,600
candle making wax		2,900
candle making uk		1,900
candle making for		1,300
beeswax candle making		1,000
candle making fragrance		590
making a candle		590
		590

PART 2 **Building**

Create the right website
Building **2**

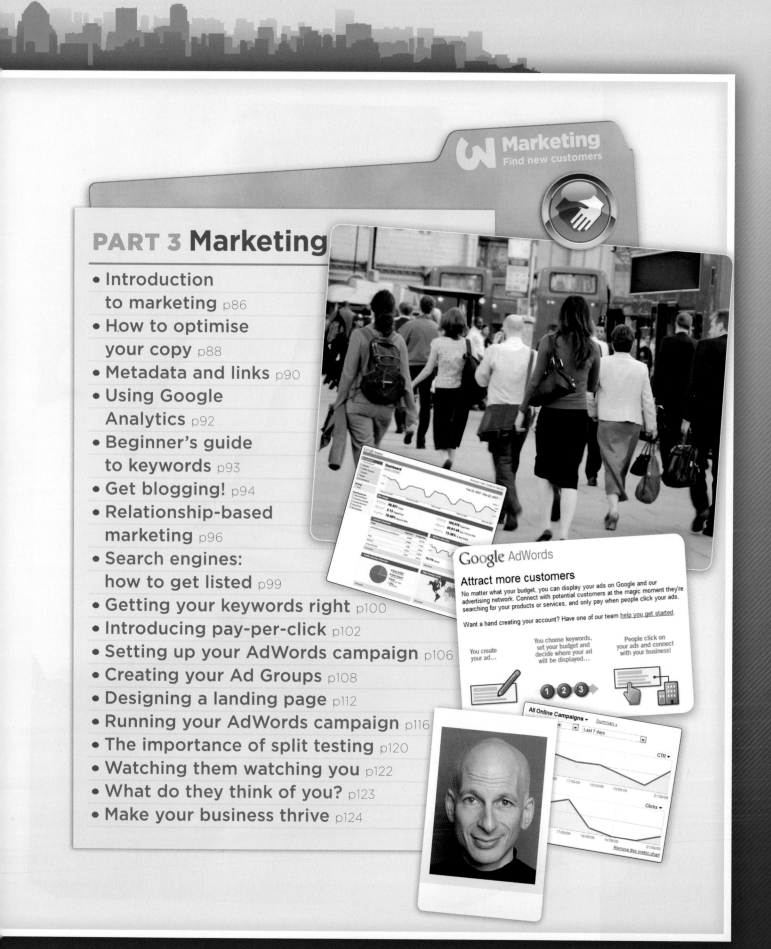

PART 3 Marketing

Marketing
Find new customers

Google AdWords

Attract more customers

No matter what your budget, you can display your ads on Google and our advertising network. Connect with potential customers at the magic moment they're searching for your products or services, and only pay when people click your ads.

Want a hand creating your account? Have one of our team help you get started.

You create your ad...

You choose keywords, set your budget and decide where your ad will be displayed...

People click on your ads and connect with your business!

1 2 3

All Online Campaigns ▾   Summary ▾

Last 7 days

CTR ▾

Clicks ▾

Remove this metric chart

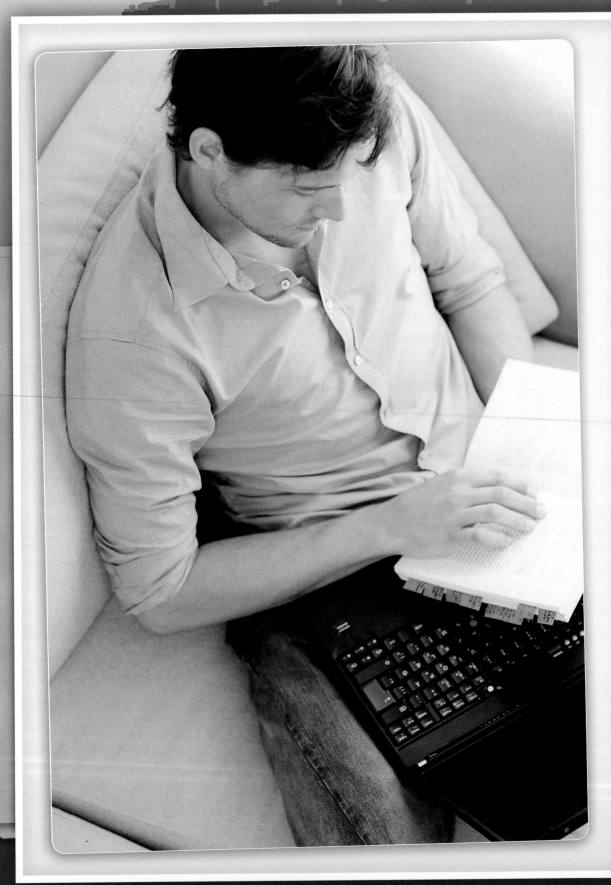

1

Planning
Start the right business

PART 1 Planning

Start the right business

Going into business

Before you begin working on your business, you need to work out what you want to get out of it. Think carefully; the answers you come up with might surprise you. Creating a business from scratch can be exciting and rewarding, but it also involves time, effort and money. So it's essential to understand why you're doing it: a clear sense of purpose will help propel you through what is likely to be a demanding process.

In many cases there will be a specific trigger that kicks this process off. In some cases it's a change in circumstances. This could be something traumatic, such as being made redundant, or even something more positive, such as coming into money.

For most people, however, the underlying reason for starting their own business is a desire for freedom. This might be the freedom to do something you enjoy; freedom from the tyranny of the corporate structure; or the freedom that money brings. There's also a natural appeal in being your own boss, especially if you're able to base your business on skills you've previously employed as part of your job. There's no doubt that working for yourself gives you a level of self-determination that simply doesn't exist within an organisation. If you have a good business, after all, you can pick and choose your clients.

consequence of this is that many people don't believe they have what it takes to start up a successful business because they're not like that.

Now, I don't doubt that such entrepreneurs exist (you can hardly get away from them on TV, after all), but I can tell you that in my ten-plus years as a business owner, the only people I've met like this have been working within blue-chip companies. Real business owners are real people. The only difference between them and people who don't work for themselves is that they have, for one reason or another, decided to go into business. There's no qualification process, there are no entry requirements – just a decision followed by action.

However, there are certain qualities that successful businesspeople tend to have. Fortunately, they're not uncommon, and all of them can be learned:

"For most people, the underlying reason for starting their own business is a desire for freedom."

 HAVE YOU GOT WHAT IT TAKES?
Think of business startups, and images of *Dragon's Den* and *The Apprentice* inevitably spring to mind. People such as Alan Sugar, Peter Jones and Deborah Meaden matched up against nervous and often self-deluded prospective entrepreneurs begging for hundreds of thousands of pounds of investment. This could hardly be further from the reality for most small-business owners.

The real problem here is the very term "entrepreneur". Thirty years ago, American businessman Michael Gerber tackled this in his book *The E-myth: Why Most Businesses Don't Work and What to Do About It*. A common perception of an entrepreneur is a smart-suited, Mercedes-driving, fast-talking, maverick risk-taker with a highly inflated view of their own self-worth. The

1 **DETERMINATION** Above all else, you need to have the stamina and drive to finish what you start. For every business that launches, I reckon a thousand expire before they see the inside of anyone's wallet.

2 **HUMILITY** Not a quality you might associate with business, but the ability to recognise that you don't know everything is essential. If you know that you don't know, you'll do your research and remain flexible enough to change direction in response to evidence. You'll also have a mind open to learning new things, every single day. Arrogance is a business-killer.

3 **DECISIVENESS** Nothing gets done unless you make decisions. Developing a business is a repeated process of information-gathering followed by decision-making. You must also be prepared to take personal responsibility for your decisions. Once you do this, you take control of your own destiny, rather than feeling dependent on the state of the economy, other people or the weather.

4 **AN ANALYTICAL MIND** You need to be able to evaluate every aspect of your business and the market in which it operates. At every stage of developing and running your business, you need to be analysing whether things are working as they should and how to improve them. The best business owners have minds that think laterally and aren't afraid to change radically the way they do things – based on good analysis, of course.

People like this don't generally make headlines. They're just quietly going about their businesses; supplying goods and services, paying taxes and providing jobs for more people than all the big corporates put together.

FROM LITTLE ACORNS Unless you're sitting on a big pile of cash, the safest way to start up a business is to run it while you're still working for someone else.

For many people, this is exactly how their business will stay: a profitable sideline and diversion from the tedium of their regular job. For others, the business will start small but their hope is to eventually grow it enough to allow them to give up the day job and run it full-time.

By starting small, you can test and adjust your product and make sure it's profitable before expanding. My aim when I'm evaluating the viability of an idea is to ask whether I think it's capable of generating £500 per month net of all costs and tax within a month or two of starting the business. This may not sound like a lot, but get a few of these going and you'll quickly earn enough to replace a full-time income. Also, a business that can generate £500 net per month can often be upscaled by increasing marketing exposure and widening the audience.

IS THIS THE RIGHT TIME? You could be forgiven for thinking that this is exactly *not* the time to start a business. However, in my view the key issue is whether *you* are ready, not the economy. The essential truth is that most businesses are poorly run, and a recession will tend to expose the weaknesses of these firms. This produces holes in the market that you – if you choose the right product or service and then implement and market it effectively – can exploit. By following the steps in this book, you'll be better prepared than the vast majority of other startups. Yes, it's true that 50% of all new businesses fail within three years. But that means that half succeed: you just need to ensure you're in the successful half.

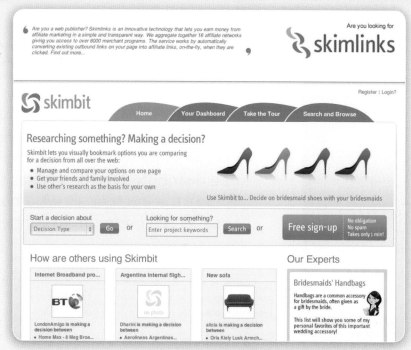

Q&A

Alicia Navarro is founder and CEO of Skimbit Ltd (www.skimbit.co.uk and www.skimlinks.com).

Q: What was the moment of inspiration for Skimbit?
A: After years of working for big companies like IBM and Vodafone, I knew I didn't want to work for a big company again. Then I got offered a job interview at Google. I didn't want the job – Google, despite its "fun factor", was very much a big company. I went for it anyway, and in the interview they asked me to come up with a business idea and say how I would market it.

I'd had the idea for Skimbit.com a while before, but it was in that moment, trying to convince Google it was a good idea, that I realised it *was* a good idea. I started the company the very next day.

Q: Lots of people have ideas for businesses but very few follow them through. What was it that enabled you to push the business through to, and beyond, launch?
A: I had nothing to lose. I didn't have a mortgage, I was single, and I'd had a burning urge to start a company all my life. I had deliberately chosen jobs that taught me the skills I would need to run a business, and at that point in my life I deliberately took a flexible job so I could work four days and have a day off to work on my business. I was willing and able to go from earning a healthy stable income to becoming a penniless entrepreneur.

I won't lie to you, it's the hardest thing I've ever done, and it isn't the right thing for many people. But the world has shown us lately that job stability is an illusion anyway. If it's in your blood to start a business, don't wait until you know everything, because you never will; but when the inspiration hits you, throw yourself completely into it.

Why an internet business?

It's one thing to decide to set up a business, but now consider the advantages of doing it online. Some have compared the advent of the internet with the invention of the printing press. In the same way that printing made books cheap enough to be distributed to the masses (at least to those who could read), the internet allows a businessperson in their broadband-connected bedroom to connect with billions of buyers.

In many ways, direct mail was the forerunner of the internet as a distribution channel, and much of the best practice established by direct marketers is still valid today. Let's take a look at the benefits of doing business online.

LOW STARTUP COSTS With both direct mail and internet, there's no need for the financial commitment of renting a shop, which reduces the risk. The costs of premises are replaced by server hosting costs; shop fittings and infrastructure by a simple electronic shopping cart; and adverts in the local press make way for Google AdWords with a worldwide audience. So the internet doesn't just lower the cost of starting up your business, it also offers an opportunity to sell to the world. Whether you take this up depends on the nature of your product and the level of your ambition.

LONG OPENING HOURS An internet business can be open 24 hours a day, 365 days a year. If you're selling a downloadable product, in fact, the sales side can take care of itself. The dream of many aspiring internet entrepreneurs is to wake up in the morning, turn on their computer and gaze adoringly at the mountain of automatically fulfilled orders as their PayPal balance grows. The promise of the internet is a business that, once set up, can be left to run itself as an efficient, low-maintenance, money-making machine. Whether it lives up to that promise is another matter.

TESTING The internet also lets you quickly and cheaply test the performance of different product lines and the effectiveness of marketing approaches. Imagine you had an idea that there was a

"The internet doesn't just lower the cost of starting up, it also offers an opportunity to sell to the world."

Passyourtheory continues to thrive while its competition has fallen away. This success is down to constant research and reinvention.

On a larger scale, Amazon is a business that could only exist online and has become one of the most famous brands in the world.

demand for 100% natural puppy-training treats. Twenty years ago your choices would boil down to either selling them yourself or finding a distributor. It clearly wouldn't be practical to rent a shop to sell one product, so you'd have to go into the general pet trade or, perhaps, hire a market stall. Finding a distributor would be little easier, involving lots of negotiations and committing to a large production run.

Fast-forward to the present day. Within a couple of weeks you can have a website up and running with a low-cost shopping cart, payment handled by PayPal, and production limited to whatever you can handle in your kitchen. If there turns out to be enough demand, you can then ramp up production, increase your marketing spend and enhance the shopping experience.

✓ **SCALE** Because of this flexibility, internet businesses can often be scaled to suit you. For example, they can be run alongside a normal job, either permanently or until you want to increase the income generated and go full-time. They can also take up much less time than traditional businesses, because so much of the work normally done by human beings is handled by software.

✓ **COMPETING WITH THE BIG BOYS** The final major benefit of the online business is that it's possible for the smallest concern to compete on more or less equal terms with global corporations. Since you have no physical shop, your customers can't necessarily tell how large your business is. A well-designed, smoothly running website can, without misleading customers, appear just as polished and trustworthy as Amazon or Tesco.

For example, 37Signals is a small team of around 15 people spread around North America. Over the past few years, it has developed a series of web-based organisational applications. These include Basecamp, the online project-management service; personal organisation software Backpack; and Highrise, a web-based contact management system. They have over three million users; 200,000 customers per employee, which isn't a bad ratio.

✗ **THE OTHER SIDE OF THE COIN** There are, of course, some downsides to doing business online. The fact you can get a business up and running quickly means your potential competitors can do the same. Indeed, the likelihood is that whatever sector you choose, there will be companies servicing it already. You're taking advantage of the fact that you can go from idea to working business in a few weeks, so you must expect others to see the same opportunity. Fortunately – and this is a theme you'll see popping up regularly throughout this book – the vast majority of your existing and future competition won't be taking the same care as you.

In enabling a new form of communication, the internet has been likened to the printing press. Now customers are easy to reach no matter where they live.

Q&A

What is PayPal?
PayPal is an internet-based payment system, owned by eBay, that can handle both tiny transactions and large ones. There is a cost involved to businesses, but not to consumers, so it's an attractive and secure way to pay for goods without the consumer having to worry about giving out their credit card details.

Think about your experiences of shopping online. My experience is that it can be like trudging through treacle. Many sites actively put barriers in the way of buying. I came across one recently that couldn't even tell me what the shipping cost of my order would be until after I'd committed to buy. Apparently they would weigh the goods when packing them and email me to let me know what it would cost to post them. Given that the most basic ecommerce packages let you incorporate shipping costs by specifying the weight of each item, this is hideously amateurish – and that company didn't get my order.

So there are opportunities in both new and existing markets to exploit the inadequate performance of competitors. My company's site, www.passyourtheory. co.uk, is an example of this. Since we launched in 2005, many others have spotted the potential for driving theory test training and have gone through the process of setting up a rival service. However, all of them have fallen by the wayside, either going out of business or ceasing advertising (usually a good sign of a business that doesn't work).

Why? Because Passyourtheory has been an ongoing project since its inception; always getting better, always learning how to market more efficiently, finding out from its customers what they want on a regular basis. Newcomers don't have this advantage – indeed, you'd be amazed at how many don't do any research at all, and the services that existed when we launched weren't doing it either. The internet gives you all the tools you need to constantly improve and reinvent your product; the issue is whether you actually do it.

What are you good at?

Before you start to generate specific ideas, it helps to look at what sort of enterprise would suit you. There's an almost infinite range of possible ventures, and the first step is to narrow these down. You owe it to yourself and your customers to build your business around your skills and interests. By working out what these are, you can both eliminate ideas that fall outside that list and use it as a springboard for generating ideas.

It's rarely a good idea to start a business that sells something you have no interest in or knowledge of. After all, you'll naturally do better when spending your time working in areas you're familiar with and interested in. Furthermore, there are a number of fundamental skills needed for all businesses. You need to be clear about which of those you have, which you can learn and which you will outsource.

We suggest using a spreadsheet to help organise your thoughts. Begin by listing your skills. Remember, a skill is something you *do* rather than something you *know*. The skills checklist opposite is by no means exhaustive, but it should get you started. Add any skill in which you think you are better than average. For example, if you keep going when others give up, you might add "stamina" to your list.

 RATE YOUR KNOWLEDGE You can now break down the skills you have into the knowledge you use to carry them out. As an example, if you've selected "Computer Programming", the knowledge that supports that skill might include PHP 5, Apache, CSS and XHTML – along with a whole raft of other, more general knowledge. For each of these aspects of your knowledge, you now need to rate your level of expertise.

Keep in mind that you should be above average on everything, since these are supposed to be your strengths. You might, therefore, choose a scale of 1 to 3, where 1 is "above average" and 3 is "exceptional".

For further inspiration, try the survey at www.authentichappiness.sas.upenn.edu. The survey you want is the VIA Signature Strengths Questionnaire. You need to answer 240 short questions, and the result will give you a real insight into what you're good at. Shaping your business around your top five strengths makes it much more likely that you will stick with it in the long run.

SKILLS EVERY BUSINESS OWNER NEEDS

Michael Gerber, author of the *E-Myth* series (www.e-myth.com), defines three roles that the business owner must fulfil: the entrepreneur, the manager and the technician. One way or another, a successful business requires all these roles. For many small businesses, all three might be fulfilled by one person (you!) – and your success will be largely determined by how well you balance the three.

THE ENTREPRENEUR is the ideas person. Without the entrepreneur, the manager and technician would have nothing to do. The entrepreneur needs to be creative, innovative and on the lookout for opportunities at all times. Did your five top VIA Signature Strengths include "Creativity" or "Judgement, critical thinking and open-mindedness"? If not, you might well need someone to help you with ideas generation. The entrepreneur has his or her eyes on the future all the time.

THE MANAGER is the organiser. The manager sets targets, organises resources, solves problems. The manager is the pragmatist and needs administrative, organisational, marketing and communication skills. In many ways the manager is the "face" of the company and is most likely to be the role that comes into contact with customers most often. Remember, all three roles might be a single person; it's a case of wearing the right hat for each situation.

THE TECHNICIAN actually gets the work done. The entrepreneur thinks up the idea; the manager puts the

> **"There are three roles that the business owner must fulfil: the entrepreneur, the manager and the technician."**

system in place and imposes deadlines; the technician builds the product. Without the entrepreneur there would be no ideas, no innovation. Without the manager, the technician would just do what he or she wanted whether or not it achieved any long-term goals. Without the technician, nothing would actually get built.

Anyone who's run a small business will probably recognise the technician in themselves more than any other. This is because most small businesses are set up by people good at something who decide they could make more money by doing it for themselves rather than an employer. The problem is that they then end up doing what they like rather than what is profitable and efficient. I've already mentioned the statistic that 50% of all businesses fail within five years. Michael Gerber would argue that this is because most businesses are "technician-driven" rather than having a balance between the three.

Action: You need to take an honest look at your list of skills and interests. Which of the skills within the three roles do you have at present, which are you prepared to learn, and which do you have no interest in?

Of the three, the manager is the easiest to outsource either to individuals (for example, your spouse) or to technology (for example, Backpack or Basecamp – more on these later in the book).

In my case, I was the typical technician. All I wanted to do was to spend days at a time coding away. However, to make a success of my businesses, I recognised the importance of the other two roles. I've therefore spent a lot of time adding to my entrepreneurial skill set, mainly through reading management books and the autobiographies of innovators. I've also developed my marketing skills through education and practice. Those skills I don't have and am not interested in – there are, after all, only so many hours in a week – I outsource.

In the first part of this book, we're focusing largely on the entrepreneur skill set as we go about identifying and assessing one or more business ideas. In the second part, the skills are largely those of the technician as we build the product and the technology to support it. In the third, the skills will be those of the manager as we market the product. A successful business depends crucially on spending time on each stage, rather than simply jumping in at stage two and hoping for the best.

Q&A

Lisa Gosling built an award-winning business (www.daisys dogdeli.co.uk) around her own skills and interests.

Q: What inspired you to start your business?
A: I am a qualified chef, so I decided to combine my two passions in life: dogs and food.
Q: What do you see as your main strengths when it comes to the business?
A: Passion and drive. You need bundles to keep you going, especially at busy times such as Christmas. Last year I baked for 36 hours without sleep!
Q: Did you originally intend the business to be your main occupation?
A: I've always worked in full-time employment, so it was a big decision to leave the security of a monthly pay cheque, but I took the plunge just over a year ago to concentrate on the deli. Best decision I ever made.
Q: What have been your main challenges?
A: Fitting everything in! There's never enough time – I always need at least another five hours in the day.
Q: What advice would you give to someone considering starting up an online business?
A: Really research every aspect. It can mount up, all the different services you need – hosting, payment gateway and so on – and you're sometimes tied into a year of payments. Also, spend as much money as you can afford on photos: I ended up wasting money trying to do it on the cheap, and it's such an important aspect of the website; customers are drawn further in by the way the first page looks.

Last but not least, before you "go live", get as many different types of people as possible to try out the website to make sure it's user-friendly.

Skills checklist

PHYSICAL
- ☐ Stamina
- ☐ Agility
- ☐ Fitness
- ☐ Building things
- ☐ Cooking
- ☐ Using machines and tools
- ☐ Gardening

ARTS
- ☐ Creativity
- ☐ Design
- ☐ Imagination

ANALYTICAL
- ☐ Logic
- ☐ Maths
- ☐ Forecasting
- ☐ Budgeting
- ☐ Administrative skills
- ☐ Setting goals
- ☐ Computer skills
- ☐ Computer programming

- ☐ Performance arts
- ☐ Improvisation
- ☐ Visual arts
- ☐ Crafts

EMOTIONAL AND INTERPERSONAL
- ☐ Teamwork and team building
- ☐ Negotiation
- ☐ Persuasion
- ☐ Listening
- ☐ Problem solving
- ☐ Customer service
- ☐ Teaching
- ☐ Coaching
- ☐ Leading
- ☐ Managing others
- ☐ Self-management
- ☐ Decisiveness

Which kind of internet business are you?

Finding out which category of business you fall into will help you shape your plans. Broadly speaking, the internet can facilitate businesses in three ways: supporting an existing bricks-and-mortar business; selling physical goods and services; and finally, selling online services and information.

Any business that doesn't have a supporting website is missing a trick. If nothing else, a well-designed site establishes credibility with your customers and tells them how to get in touch with you. Note that qualification: the site must be well designed, or at the very least it mustn't look as though it's fallen out of a £10 "build a site in a minute" box from PC World or been put together in PowerPoint using every available font and colour.

Many businesses depend entirely on the internet. It's the world's biggest product catalogue, and the majority of ecommerce is now conducted through companies who have no physical shop front.

SELLING GOODS It's in the selling of physical goods that the real-world benefits of using the internet as a marketing channel become so obvious. For example, if you wanted to set up your own small supermarket, there's no way you could compete with the integrated systems – both electronic, physical and marketing – that the big players such as Tesco now employ. The cost of fitting out a store in an attractive way, adding the stock management and EPOS (electronic point of sale) systems and then employing enough staff is a huge investment that excludes almost everyone.

Compare this with setting up an online retailer. All the infrastructure – including stock management, product display and payment processing – can be purchased or rented at a low price. This makes it perfectly possible to give your visitors (almost) as effective an experience as they might have at, say, Play.com. Indeed, with services such as eBay shops and Amazon Marketplace, you can use the infrastructure of these companies to sell your products. That so few small online retailers actually create efficient sales processes is a pity, but it opens up gaps that you can exploit.

However, simply putting together a slick, efficient "sales funnel" (the process from choosing a product to paying for it) is not nearly enough to ensure success. If the product isn't right, the best shop in the world won't succeed: what having the right software does ensure is that you don't lose sales you should otherwise get.

Working with – or being – a web developer to create your own site from scratch (left) means you can make it more distinctive and professional than a ready-made shopfront within a service such as eBay (above). The result should be a more personal and compelling experience for your customers.

SELLING DOWNLOADS AND ONLINE
SERVICES The advent of the internet, and specifically broadband, has given rise to a whole range of new commercial products. The internet itself is the natural home for these, and in many ways they represent the ideal online business. Having no physical products means you don't need to buy any stock, store it or dispose of it if it doesn't sell. It becomes possible to keep an enormous range of products at no cost.

In fact, a whole new economy has been built around this "long tail", in which it's possible to make money by selling tiny quantities of thousands of different items, adding up to profitable revenue. Amazon is the most obvious case in point: it makes much of its profit from obscure books that aren't found in high-street bookshops.

There's also a huge market for online services. 37Signals (www.37signals.com) has made an entire business out of providing online organisational software, including its flagship Basecamp project-management service. Online accounting software FreeAgent (www.freeagentcentral. com) is, in my view, the most elegant UK-developed web application. Like Basecamp, FreeAgent is one of those rare software products that has radically altered how I work: in this case it has reduced the length of time it takes to keep my accounts up to date by around 90%.

You might also use the internet to sell your own internet-related skills. For example, if you're a copywriter, web designer or Google AdWords specialist, you'll use a website to sell your services. This can be similar to the website of a bricks-and-mortar business, but will need to be much more sophisticated and to reflect current trends, because as well as being a brochure it's a living, working example of your abilities. If you're a web developer, for example, you'd better make sure your site looks good. If you're an AdWords specialist, you'd better have an effective AdWords campaign of your own and plenty of further examples online.

Identifying the nature of your business is a crucial step in putting together your plan.

> **"A new economy has been built around making money by selling tiny quantities of thousands of items."**

Organisational tools such as 37Signals' Basecamp can help the smallest of businesses work efficiently enough to rival much larger companies.

SELLING INFORMATION
Enrol in almost any internet marketing guru's training course, and one method of making money will be pushed more than any other: information products.

These really do have a lot going for them. Usually created in the form of PDFs (such as eBooks), MP3s (such as seminars) or videos (the sky's the limit), they tend to be products that can then be sold for years with minimal change. They can be very quick to get into place, and they can be naturally slotted into Google's search engine so that you know the people visiting your site are actually looking for the information you want to sell.

Having said that, information products have their problems. The most fundamental of these is that web users increasingly expect information to be free. To charge for a product, you need to convince potential customers you can offer information that's not freely available elsewhere and that you're an expert in the relevant field.

One of my sites, www.passyourtheory.co.uk, can justify charging for access to our materials because the driving theory test database and hazard perception clips are licensed from the government's Driving Standards Agency and require a contract between the service provider and the Department of Transport. For the learner driver, therefore, the only place to get this information online is via a licensed provider who will charge for the privilege (and pay the DSA a royalty in return).

Our UK citizenship test site, on the other hand, failed because the information it sold could be found elsewhere. Furthermore, the expectations of your potential customers are getting more sophisticated, so the cost and time required to create your materials is going to be greater.

However, if you have specialist knowledge that you believe others will pay for – after all, this is the proposition behind most books, including the one you're reading now – then an information business can be easy to set up and highly profitable.

GOING YOUR OWN WAY Given the sophisticated systems and ease of setup offered by eBay and Amazon, why would you want to go your own way and set up your own independent website?

The first and most important reason is that you get complete control of the setup, configuration and marketing of your site and its ecommerce software. For some businesses, this could be seen as a disadvantage – a barrier preventing you from simply getting started. If you wanted to start a business selling second-hand books, for example, Amazon Marketplace is the perfect platform to use. The margins per item are likely to be pretty low, but you get high-quality infrastructure, guaranteed traffic and specialised stock-management tools. ➡

NeoBudget, an online personal finance service, uses the Spreedly customer service system to handle its recurring subscriptions.

→ However, for many product types, the choice is between an eBay shop and one of your own (or, indeed, evolving from one to the other, or even maintaining both). There's only so much customisation you can do to an eBay shop, and whatever you do, your shop will never feel like an entirely independent entity either to yourself or your customers. A substantial business will achieve greater credibility by appearing to be more professional and by being able to offer greater functionality with its own site – though exceptions will apply.

Daisy's Dog Deli (www.daisysdogdeli.co.uk) is a case in point. Compare the home page (see p14) with the Holistic Pet World store on eBay (also on p14). Although both are functional, I know which one I think looks more credible and professional. Lisa Gosling, creator of Daisy's Dog Deli, has been able to customise the design to suit her business, decide what additional information to include, and choose which ecommerce partner to work with; in this case, Actinic Express. Lisa's options when it comes to online marketing are much wider than if she had an eBay shop, as is her ability (or that of her web developer) to optimise the site for Google searches.

By creating your own site, you can implement a more sophisticated marketing strategy. When we get into Part 3 of this book, you'll see why this is so important.

PAYMENT SOLUTIONS If you create a software product or download, you can either integrate your own shopping cart in a similar way to selling a physical product or you can use a specialist third party. Digital River's share-it offers a complete ecommerce and delivery system. You can either have share-it store your software and supply a link to the purchaser or store it on your own server. Many different shopping carts include some support for downloadable products, but systems such as share-it offer sophisticated features such as registration key generation and trial versions, so if you're selling software there's little reason to look elsewhere. Costs range from 4.9% to 8.9%. You'll need your own website to publicise your product and act as a link into the share-it system. This is also the case with information products and online services. An information product can be delivered using most standard ecommerce products, but billing for an online service is rather more complicated.

Most online services are paid for on a rolling basis, usually monthly, so your payment system needs to take account of this. For most service providers, this has traditionally meant writing their own recurring billing software, which is hideously complicated. The system needs to handle refunds, pro-rata payments, trial periods and changes of payment details along with a whole host of less usual occurrences – and this, on its own, is one of the major barriers between a great idea for an online service and its realisation. In fact, there's a significant danger that the subscription management system could take longer to perfect than the online service itself.

"You have a choice between an eBay shop and one of your own. A business will achieve greater credibility with its own site."

However, a new service called Spreedly (www.spreedly.com) offers a solution by sitting between your service and a range of payment providers and handling repeated billing for you. Once integrated into your website, Spreedly will present the subscription options to your customer and you'll be able to retrieve that customer's current subscription status using the Spreedly API (the "application programming interface" that lets you connect a solution to your own software). While this isn't a simple process, it's much easier than doing it from scratch. At the time of writing, Spreedly costs $700 to get started, plus a $19-per-month fee and a transaction commission of around 1%. This may seem expensive, but $700 wouldn't go far if you had to develop a system all by yourself.

Amember.com is a cheaper alternative. For a one-off fee of $200, it offers a series of PHP scripts that handle payment-processing and give access to member-only pages. It's not as flexible or sophisticated as Spreedly, but it's been around for much longer, supports most payment gateways and has good support. This is the system to choose if you have a membership site that works by allowing access to protected content to subscribers only.

Shops that sell for you

eBay

If you've decided to sell a physical product, you have two main choices when it comes to how you supply the infrastructure. The first is to hook into an existing provider's system. This is how eBay shops work: as an eBay "shop owner", you are simultaneously adding your goods to the search-based interface used by most shoppers, while also having a more traditional catalogue-style shop that your customers can browse.

The advantages of having an eBay shop, compared with listing each product individually, include the credibility, and thus the trust, they generate. Buyers are more likely to buy from a business than from a private individual, particularly for higher-value items. Your shopfront further reinforces this and makes it more likely that you'll get follow-up sales as buyers browse your shop.

All this results in a potentially increased conversion rate: the percentage of visitors who end up buying. Again, of course, it depends on exactly what you're selling.

The cost of running an eBay shop is a minimum £14.99 per month rental. You then pay an insertion fee and final value fee, all of which are very similar to the prices paid by private sellers for standard auction sales. However, you get a big discount on "Buy It Now" listings, where any buyer who decides to pay the stated price wins the item immediately, without having to wait for an auction to play out. Given that most shops operate almost entirely using this type of listing, big savings can be made.

You'll still need to sell a fair amount to recover your monthly rental in savings. However, if you decided to build your own site, you'd probably need to hire your ecommerce system, and the monthly eBay rental compares quite favourably with that expense.

Finally, along with eBay's fees you'll also be charged by PayPal for processing your customers' payments. All this needs to be borne in mind when you price your products.

As an example, let's say you want to sell a CD with a "Buy It Now" price of £9.99. You would pay an insertion fee of 10p and, if sold, a 9.9% Final Value Fee (99p). Then there's PayPal's processing fee of 3.4% + 20p: 54p in this case. So, ignoring any profit to be made on postage and packing, assuming you had only a single picture for the item, ignoring any VAT implications and not taking into account your rental fee, you'd be left with £8.36 net.

Amazon

Amazon's Marketplace offers many of the same advantages as the eBay shop system, but works in an entirely different way. First, you can only sell items that already appear in the Amazon system. This makes the process of adding items simple and intuitive: you simply search for the product in the usual way and click the "I have one to sell" button. You then specify its condition and set a price (Amazon Marketplace is not an auction).

Amazon charges a "completion fee" of 86p per item plus a "closing fee" of 17.25% of the sales price. Bear in mind that this includes what you would otherwise pay out as a payment processing fee, as Amazon uses its own system. Finally, Amazon also takes a "variable closing fee", which is deducted from the postage price that the buyer pays, the remainder going to you as a postage credit.

As an example, let's say you've sold a book at £9.99. You'll pay an 86p completion fee, a £1.72 closing fee and a 49p variable closing fee. However, you'll be credited with £2.75 to cover postage, leaving £9.67. Given that you only have to send books by second-class post, and this might cost less than £1, so – as with eBay – you can make a profit on that as well.

This explains why you'll see paperbacks advertised at 1p. The seller is paying only the completion fee and the variable closing fee, and making a profit on the postage. But you need to sell an awful lot to make that pay.

Businesses will want a Pro Merchant account. This has a £28.75 monthly fee (£25 if you're VAT registered), but the completion fee is waived, making it worthwhile if you sell more than 30 items per month. You also get inventory management tools to help upload and edit stock details.

> **"Buyers are more likely to buy from a business than from a private individual. Your shop-front reinforces this and makes it more likely you'll get follow-up sales."**

Coming up with your business idea

It's time to come up with that million-dollar idea. And it's all about you. Having gone through the exercise on pp12-13, you should by now have identified what you're good at. The extra dimension you need to add is how much each of these areas of skill or expertise really appeals to you.

In most cases, you'll probably find that those things you're particularly good at also happen to interest you, but it's important to put both of these factors together to arrive at a list of potential opportunities. Your chances of establishing a successful business are much, much greater if you develop it based on your skills and interests.

Let's take an example. In my case, "creativity" is at the top of my VIA Signature Strengths (see p12). I also think I'm good at making things, cooking and gardening. Immediately, then, I'm thinking about businesses that involve creating things. This might be a business that creates things itself, or a business that enables others to create those things. For instance, my love of cooking might push me towards opening a restaurant or starting a business developing recipes to help people produce wonderful food for themselves.

I also notice that no-one is advertising in Google with those keywords. If you see this in your own results, it's worth keeping a note, as this can mean one of two things: either there's no market, or you've spotted a market that no-one else has been able to exploit yet. Food for thought – pardon the pun – either way.

TURN ON THE RADAR In my view, most of the best business ideas come out of frustrations or opportunities spotted in everyday life. The idea for Passyourtheory.co.uk came about when standing in the queue in WH Smith behind someone buying a driving theory test CD-ROM. It suddenly occurred to me that it must be possible to offer this service online. The candle-making business idea came out of my extreme

"If no-one is advertising with your keywords, either there's no market, or you've spotted a market no-one else has exploited."

It may be that your own list of strengths doesn't immediately cause an idea to leap to mind. That's fine, because the purpose of this list is to make sure the ideas you do come up with fit in with what you're good at and what interests you.

One technique for generating business ideas is simply to Google your interests. If I Google "creative cooking", I get results including www.creativecook.co.uk (a spice company), creative cooking holidays, menu suggestions for men, ethnic cooking ideas and even how to cook creatively for people with medical conditions.

McDonald's Ray Kroc didn't invent burgers, but he saw a better way to run an existing business.

disappointment at the quality and cost of the retail kit I bought. Similarly, 37Signals' Basecamp product came out of their frustration, as a web design agency, with the email ping-pong that characterises web development projects.

Ray Kroc, founder of McDonald's, so admired the efficient way in which schoolchildren could turn out identical burgers like clockwork that he bought out Dick and Mac McDonald and established the biggest restaurant franchise in the world. Now, I'm not suggesting you'll necessarily want to take the approach of buying out an existing company (although, if done with care, that can be very successful), but you can be aware of what one company does well and apply it to another industry. Indeed, the McDonald's principle has been applied to many other businesses with great success.

Planning
Start the right business

I call this phase "turning on the radar", and it's more a frame of mind than anything else. For the next few weeks, critically analyse every commercial interaction you have. Look out especially for those that frustrate or disappoint you. Don't overanalyse, don't eliminate any at this point: the aim is to get a list of ideas to work on.

BRAINSTORMING We're all familiar with the technique of brainstorming, although it's rarely practised properly. The idea is to put analysis of the suggestions completely on hold at this point and simply generate ideas. Your skills and interests would be a good starting point. Contrary to popular belief, in my view, this is best done on your own. Human nature being what it is, it's next to impossible not to react to someone else's "stupid" idea, and this inhibits the process. The purpose here is to generate as many ideas as possible and not to allow snap judgements or instant decisions to veto them.

Here are the ideas I came up with at the end of my idea-generation phase:

1 A daily Sudoku puzzle emailed to each customer's inbox every morning for printing

2 A "garden in a bucket" kit for people with limited garden space

3 A service to help migrants to the UK to pass their citizenship exams

4 A business selling kits enabling buyers to make their own candles

EVALUATING YOUR IDEAS The mistake many, many business owners make is to fasten on to the first or most obvious idea and build a business around that. This is hugely risky, and is probably the main reason behind the high failure rate among small businesses: if your product doesn't have an audience, it doesn't matter how well you run your company or market the product, it will fail.

Equally, if you've generated a lot of ideas, there's no point in subjecting them all to a full market analysis, or you might end up wasting so much time that you never actually get started. So, as a first step, you need to apply the following criteria to your crop of business ideas:

CAN YOU MAKE MONEY AT IT? This may seem like a banal, obvious question, but you must honestly and objectively feel that there is a market for your idea. Unless you are truly confident that there is a market, reject the idea right now – however emotionally attached to it you might be. ➜

Affiliate schemes

You don't always need an original idea. One option is to find someone who's already operating in a market and become an affiliate. Typically, this involves creating and publicising a website that drives traffic to your partner. You receive a percentage of each sale. In a sense, this works in the opposite way to the traditional approach of developing businesses around what frustrates you about existing offerings: in this case you're looking for examples of excellent products and services.

You might imagine you'd find it irritating to be promoting someone else's product, but this is a quick and relatively painless way to start, and some schemes are extremely generous. The only cost to you (apart from web hosting) is marketing, usually via Google AdWords, and this can be controlled at a very fine level of detail.

Expert eye

Larry Heiman, Senior E-Myth Business Coach (www.e-myth.com), says your business should be built around your "Primary Aim".

"YOUR PRIMARY AIM IS YOUR DEFINITION OF yourself – the qualities you manifest when you're at your best. As coaches, we often describe it as your 'personal bumper sticker'. The Primary Aim is the process of finding the words to describe that essence of who you are; the source of your passion and drive.

"Once you have discovered your Primary Aim, your business should be a vehicle to nurture and fulfill that passion. Maybe there is something in the nature of the business itself that directly feeds that passion, so showing up every day completes the circuit. Or it may be that the business is simply the source of the fuel to provide you with the time, energy and wherewithal to be more completely living as your best self.

"Just as your business is a vehicle for your Primary Aim, the force of the Primary Aim is what drives you to visualise and build the business that will allow you to truly live your passion. It allows you the ability to put your life in perspective and helps you make conscious choices that are consistent with what is most important to you."

Planning
Start the right business

1

Focus on what your potential customers are worth over a full 12 months. For example, a Basic plan on Basecamp is worth an initial payment of only £14.50, but over a year the customer will pay £175. This makes all the difference in the world to your marketing budget!

→ Do you personally know people who'd buy your product or service? Do you know that lots of people might use it? For example, in the case of www.passyourtheory.co.uk, it was obvious that there was a big potential market since I knew that lots of people take their driving test every year. Other "good ideas" I've had don't pass this test: indeed, for every ten ideas, I only proceed to analyse one of them.

Action: Reject all ideas that you're not confident will make money – even if you love them.

? HOW MUCH IS EACH CUSTOMER WORTH? Think about how the pricing of your product or service is likely to work. How much income can you expect from each customer per annum? If at all possible, pick a product or service that means you can establish a long-term relationship with your customers. You want to be able to sell repeatedly to them, since it's much cheaper to sell to existing customers than to find new ones.

As a general rule of thumb, you should be looking for an income of between £25 and £100 per customer per year. Why? Because it's almost always a mistake to try to occupy the low end of any market and compete on price alone. Remember, the income you're looking for is spread over a whole year, and knowing that your typical customer is worth, say, £100 per year means that your marketing budget can be set with this in mind. If your typical sale is only £10, you may baulk at the idea of spending £10 in AdWords

to attract that customer; but if you anticipate that the customer will then go on to spend another £90 in the first year, that £10 investment looks a bargain.

How do you know how much a customer will be worth? The simplest way is to look at any existing services: pick a value in the mid-range to get the level of a single sale.

Action: Reject all ideas that won't generate at least £25 per annum per customer. Be very wary of any idea that involves a single sale with no follow-ons.

? CAN YOU SUM IT UP IN A SENTENCE? The famous "elevator pitch" is a great way of establishing if you have a focused, sellable business idea. Unless you can summarise your idea in a single sentence, you should be wary. First, you must communicate your business and what it offers in the limited space available in Google AdWords. Second, your website will get just a few seconds to grab a visitor's interest before they head elsewhere: it's rare that a potential customer who doesn't immediately "get it" hangs around long enough to buy.

Action: Reject any idea that can't be summed up in a single sentence.

.com

to the World's largest Web Host

Over 9 million customers have spoken. Thank you for your loyalty and trust which have helped make us the leading web host worldwide!

For over 20 years 1&1 has provided cutting edge services and products to millions of users. A total of over 70,000 servers run in our state-of-the-art data centres. We utilise green energy and the latest technology to ensure that the high-security, speed and power demands of your website are met with ease.

1&1 invests in the future, we develop new technologies, are financially stable and dependable and will be hosting your website for many years to come!

DOMAINS

.com

BEST OFFERS IN THE UK

~~£8.99 per year~~

£4.99 first year*

WEB HOSTING

GET 3 MONTHS FREE*

Powerful hosting solutions for small to medium business sites.

1&1 Business Package
- NEW: 20 GB Web Space
- NEW: UNLIMITED Traffic
- 3 FREE .uk domains included

~~£8.99 per month~~

£0.00 for 3 months*

HURRY, OFFERS END 31/12/2009!

.co.uk, .me.uk, .org.uk domains now only £2.49 first year*

*Terms and conditions apply, please see website for further details. Get 3 months free on selected web hosting packages when you sign up for a 1 year package! Special offers available as of 01/11/2009 and for a limited time only. Prices exclude VAT.

1&1

MEMBER OF
united internet

Call **0871 641 21 21** Calls cost 6p per minute from a BT landline, calls from other operators and mobiles may be higher.

or visit us now **www.1and1.co.uk**

Your business 0.1

It's possible that you'll reach this stage with no viable ideas left. That's fine – you've just saved yourself a fortune by eliminating your non-commercial business concepts. You now need to go back to the drawing board, give it a little time, and generate some more ideas to put through the same process.

Assuming you do have an idea or two left: well done. It's now time to give your nascent business a name. Isn't this a bit premature? After all, your more detailed research might still rule this business out before it even launches. However, your business name is essential to your marketing, so you need to know it before you can evaluate the size of the potential market.

Begin by looking at your "elevator pitch". Here's mine for the candle-making business:

"A business selling high-quality, reusable and customisable candle-making kits to beginners."

Your elevator pitch will give you some initial Google search keywords that your potential customers will find you with. Indeed, if you've got it right, your one-sentence description should give you the most important keywords straight away. If not, are you sure it truly describes your business?

My prime keywords are "candle-making", "kits", "beginners" and "high-quality", in roughly that order of importance. Because of the way Google works, both in its "natural" search listings (those that aren't paid for) and AdWords (sponsored listings), you're automatically rewarded if your domain name includes the search terms used by your potential visitor. This manifests itself as a higher natural ranking for your site and/or lower AdWords costs.

The practical consequence of this is that your business domain name must include your most important keywords, and it also makes sense to name the business itself the same way. "What about Amazon?" I hear you cry. Neither its company name nor domain name include the word "book", after all. But stand by for a reality check: you *aren't* Amazon! Don't make your life more difficult by working against Google.

In my case, I settled on www.makingyourown candles.co.uk. My personal preference is for my domain names, where possible, to include a verb. So why not "makeyourowncandles"? That would have been easier on the ear, but remember, my keywords are "candle *making*".

The other ideas from my list that have made it this far are www.freesudoku.co.uk and www.gardeninginabucket.co.uk. Let's see how many survive the next stage.

Planning
Start the right business
1

Case study 1: The idea

If you've read the introduction to this book, you'll already know that while writing it I created a real, functioning online business, which you can see at www.makingyourowncandles.co.uk. This idea came about when I bought a candle-making kit from a major craft-product retailer and was massively disappointed by the contents.

The product cost £11 and I estimated, after a little research, that the contents would have cost the manufacturer around £1.25. The fact that such kits exist at all is prima facie evidence of a market, so it ticks that box. Given the retail cost of the kits, it's not unreasonable to expect to be able to make £25 or more per year from the initial purchase and refills.

The "elevator pitch" is simple enough: a business selling high-quality, reusable and customisable candle-making kits to beginners. From that, I can generate my Google keywords and choose my domain name: www.makingyourowncandles.co.uk.

The idea for my business came from the shortcomings of a candle-making kit that I bought for my own use.

Is there a market for your business idea?

You've come up with some ideas: now you need to see if the market is there. It doesn't have to be huge, because you can succeed by hitting the right niche. The internet has many unique properties, but one of the most important is that it opens up a truly global market to anyone with a product or service.

Planning Start the right business

The consequence of this is that products that wouldn't be viable within a single town, region or even country may have a big enough audience across the world. Some, of course, are specific to a country – PassYourTheory being one – and it's rarely a good idea to go global from the start, since marketing will need a different approach in each territory. Attempting to reach too broad a market too early is one of the prime reasons for online business failure, as your cash disappears into the Google AdWords black hole.

YOUR NICHE The specific market you're targeting is your "niche". You should have some product or service ideas by now, and the next step is to consider who, exactly, is likely to be your target audience. This is an inexact science at this stage, since to some extent you can't predict exactly who is going to be attracted to your service or product enough to buy it. However, it should be possible to get a reasonable idea, which you can then amend as your business grows.

Remember, you should already believe that your business can make at least £25 per customer per annum and is based on your own skills and interests. You should also have your one-line "elevator pitch".

SO WHO IS IT AIMED AT? Think about your market and specifically look at:

1 The likely age range
2 Whether they're more likely to be male or female, or if there's no gender preference
3 Their interests and, most importantly, what other websites they're likely to visit

---

> Web Show options...   Results 1 - 10 of about 235,000
>
> **Litter Training your Rabbit**
> Litter Training Your Rabbit by Emma Magnus MSc. Over the past few years an increasing number of people have moved away from the traditional idea of keeping ...
> www.apbc.org.uk/article7.htm - Cached - Similar
>
> **How to Train a Rabbit - wikiHow**
> If you want to teach your rabbit to come when called, start her training by ... Avoid overfeeding your rabbit during training sessions, and avoid using ...
> www.wikihow.com/Train-a-Rabbit - Cached - Similar
>
> **Training Your Rabbit with a Trio of Tricks - For Dummies**
> If you let your rabbit run in a large area of the house, you may want her to come when you call her name. It will allow you to find her if she's hiding and ...
> www.dummies.com/how-to/content/training-your-rabbit-with-a-trio-of-tricks.html - Cached - Similar
>
> **Rabbit Training** - barneyandjemima.co.uk
> How to train your rabbit: Toilet litter box training and behaviour training.
> www.barneyandjemima.co.uk/training.html - Cached - Similar

If you have an idea for a rabbit-training product, there doesn't seem to be much competition. But is there a market for it?

Your product or service needs to be marketed in such a way that it feels natural to your target audience. If you personally represent that audience fairly well, look at the sites you visit on a regular basis. Look at the site design, language and graphics used and how they achieve a sale.

SIZE ISN'T (THAT) IMPORTANT It is possible to select a market that's too big. You'll find it hard to target your marketing and you'll be competing with large companies. You should be looking for a niche that, while it's big enough to sustain a business, is small enough to provide an opportunity for you to dominate. Even with a global market, some niches are too small to be worthwhile, and the purpose of this stage is to work out where your business fits.

YOU DON'T HAVE TO BE ORIGINAL One of the great myths that prevents many people from starting their

---

"Aim to find the weaknesses of your rivals and provide an experience at least as professional as the best big-name competitor."

own business is that you need a completely novel idea. Looking at a market, it's easy to feel intimidated by the competition. After all, these companies must be doing something right, surely? Not at all. The fact is that most businesses are poorly run, whether in terms of their core product, marketing, management, customer service or the conversion process. In difficult economic times, such businesses get weeded out as they cut down on marketing and product development (the very things that improve your chances of success), thus leaving gaps for you.

The key is to be better than your competition. In some markets this is easier than others, and the only way to find this out is to evaluate the quality of your competitors. You can make money by being better than your rivals if you:

1 Have a better product or service
2 Do better marketing
3 Offer supreme customer service
4 Produce at a lower cost

I recommend concentrating on the first two in this list. Unless customer service is built into your product and measurable (for example, if you're a delivery firm), it's hard to convince potential customers that your service is much better than their existing supplier – phrases such as "passionate about customer service" have been paid lip service too often by big corporations.

Producing at a lower cost is also something to avoid if at all possible; it's certainly not the basis of any business I'd be involved in. Margins are squeezed, and you're vulnerable to a big player coming into the market and undercutting you due to economies of scale.

You have the best possible chance of success if your product or service is measurably better than the competition and you employ better marketing techniques.

CHECK OUT THE COMPETITION You should know your main keywords as part of the process of coming up with a business name. Google them and see what comes up in the sponsored listings. Only pay attention to the first page, as this is where the real competition is.

Look at the ads. You're mainly interested in those that include the keywords you typed within their body, title and domain name. These ads have probably been created by a marketer who knows at least the basics of Google AdWords optimisation. Take a look at their website. Do they *only* sell a product or service like yours, or is it one of a big range? If you find a market where no-one is concentrating on selling a product like yours, but where many sell such a product alongside others, give that product a big tick.

Spend some time getting to know the sites and, specifically, the shopping process, of your competitors.

Case study
2: Search check

My main key phrase is "candle-making kit". Typing this into Google, I can see the number one position in the Sponsored Listings is occupied by Fred Aldous (a bricks-and-mortar craft retailer) with an ad that is not optimised and is therefore likely to be expensive. In the number two position is a general online craft retailer. Number three is a US-based craft retailer. Due to the cost of shipping heavy wax, this is unlikely to be a competitor.

Number four, bizarrely, is a Swedish castle specialising in weddings; heaven only knows which of my keywords triggered that! Number five is Amazon. Finally, number six is a gift retailer (and a potential supplier of our candle kits).

You'll also notice the Product Search results summarised above the natural listings. These are added by submitting your product to Google's Merchant Center (www.google.com/merchants). If you can achieve a high rank here, you're getting a lot of visibility for nothing.

My main conclusion from this is that none of my competitors is running a site dedicated solely to candle making (let alone candle-making kits), although there are companies selling kits among a range of products. These tend to be the cheap products that inspired MakingYourOwnCandles.co.uk, so there could well be a market for a higher-quality version supplied by us.

Given all this, it should be possible to create a highly optimised Google campaign, focused entirely on candle-making kits, that won't cost the Earth.

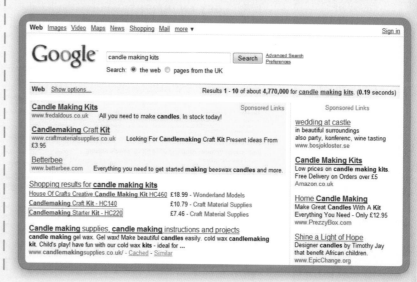

Concentrate first on the good-quality ads, identified using the criteria we described just now, but also take a look at those that appear in the top two positions in the Google results. It is possible to get a top position with a poor ad simply by paying a lot, so positions one and two are often occupied by big names. Take a look at this phase in our case study, above, for an example analysis.

Your aim is to find the weaknesses of your rivals so that you can provide an experience that is at least as professional as the best big-name competitor while being focused, personal and mercilessly efficient.

Analysing the market and the competition

As we've said, no matter what type of business you intend to set up, it's vital to analyse whether there's a market for your product or service and who's already in that market. But how? The simplest way is to estimate the number of Google searches that people are initiating for the relevant keywords.

Too many searches suggests your keywords are too broad and competition is likely to be fierce. Too few and the market might not be big enough. All you need to count them is a Google account. If you don't have one, sign up at www.google.co.uk: click Sign in, then Create an Account.

① **GET AN INSIGHT** Go to www.google.com/insights/search to start Google Insights. This shows how search terms compare in terms of traffic over time as a percentage of total searches. To see this in practice, type in your two or three most important

keyword phrases, set your regional options to reflect your intended market, and click Search.

In my example, "candle making" has roughly five times more search volume than "candle making kits", but they tend to peak at the same time. The peak in April 2009 is in all likelihood due to the TV programme *Kirstie's Homemade Home*, in which Kirstie Allsopp made candles for her new house. Overall, the trend for both has been slightly negative until this year when, perhaps surprisingly, both have begun to trend upwards. One word of warning: remember the peaks and troughs are as a *percentage* of

1

3

4

Google AdWords' Keyword tool gives you a rough idea of how many people will click on your advert and what it will cost you.

overall searches. They don't tell you whether the actual number of searches has risen or fallen, but rather whether your topics are relatively gaining or losing popularity. In this case, I'm happy they're holding up well over time.

2 **THE KEYWORD IS ADWORDS** We'll use the Google AdWords Keyword tool to estimate the number of clicks we'll get when we advertise. You need a Google AdWords account for this: see p103 to create it. Once you've signed up, go to the Keywords tool and type in the same keyword phrases you used for Insights.

The principle of Google AdWords is that you pay for your ad to appear in the Sponsored Listings whenever people search for a given keyword. Rather than paying a fixed fee up front, you pay each time a user clicks on your ad. (This takes the user to your own website, where it's up to you to persuade them to buy your product or service.)

The Keywords tool helps you see how this will work in practice. Enter some words, click Get Keyword Ideas and Google will present a list. Add those that seem appropriate to your list by clicking Add. The bar under "Advertiser Competition" shows how competitive each keyword phrase is. You needn't eliminate those where the bar is full or nearly full, but make sure you add any where the bar is empty or nearly empty, since you're likely to be able to advertise using those keywords for very little money.

Also bear in mind the estimates of search volume (local or global, depending on your target market). In very round terms, you want between 15,000 and 30,000 searches across your keywords if you're advertising in the UK, and 50,000 to 75,000 if you're advertising in the UK and US. Clearly, this depends on your specific product and its price level, but you're unlikely to want to bother with a product that generates 100 searches a month; equally, a market that gets a million searches is probably too big for you.

3 **CHANCES OF SUCCESS** Now click Estimate Search Traffic. The next page shows the expected number of clicks (times that users will click on your ad if you sign up for this keyword), the cost per click, and the position you'll appear in the Sponsored Listings. This is in contrast to the number of searches, which you saw on the previous screen. These figures need to be treated with extreme caution, since the actual percentage of searchers who end up clicking on your ad will depend on the quality of the ad. Increase the cost per click (CPC) value until all the keywords are predicted to appear at positions 1 to 3. This will give you a rough guide to what your competitors are paying to appear in those positions in the search results.

4 **YOU PAYS YOUR MONEY...** Now adjust the value down until you see the ads predicted to

appear at positions 4 to 6. This will indicate what you might pay to appear on the first page of the results.

These figures are very, *very* rough. However, if they suggest, for example, that you'd need to pay £5 per click to achieve a front-page position for your £9.99 product, you might want to think again. Every time a potential customer clicks on your ad, you'll pay Google this amount; the average profit you expect to make out of that customer – taking into account that most people who click the ad won't end up buying anything at all – needs to justify that outlay.

On the other hand, if you can get a front-page position for 10p per click, things are looking rosy: this means competition in your market is not so intense that there's no room for you to start a viable business. In my case, it looks as though I will be able to pay around 10p to achieve a front-page advert for both the keywords "candle making" and "candle-making kit".

I expect a conversion rate for a first sale to any particular customer of around 5%, so I need 20 visitors to make one sale. At 10p, that means my marketing will cost approximately £2 to generate that first sale, and I can now use that figure in working out my costs. Future sales to the same customer will, of course, cost much less.

With www.makingyourowncandles.co.uk, then, Google suggests that I can expect around 100,000 searches per month. I would expect around 5% of those searchers to visit my website, so that's 5,000 visitors. Approximately 5% of these (250) will buy from me as a first-time customer. Clearly, if any of those figures change, the end results could be completely different – but it looks as though there might be a viable market there.

Enter the keywords you think are relevant to your business, and Google will generate more that you may want to investigate. The great benefit here is that everything is based on real search data.

Ask them what they want!

When it comes to running a business, you can't base decisions on gut instinct. You need to find out the triggers that will make prospective customers buy. Too many would-be entrepreneurs tear headlong into business without doing the most basic market research. You've now established that there's a market for your idea, but that doesn't tell you enough about exactly what sort of product or service will do well in that market.

Larry Heiman (pictured left), senior business coach for E-Myth Worldwide (www.e-myth.com), says: "A successful prospective business owner needs to know who their customers are and what they must do to satisfy them as completely as possible, and be able to do so consistently." Fortunately, there's an absurdly simple way of finding out exactly what shape your product should take in order to sell: *Ask your potential customers.*

The classic way of doing this is with the "Three question survey" popularised by Glenn Livingstone (www.glennlivingstone.com). Three questions may not seem a lot but, well chosen, they can ensure you head in the right direction with your product development; and the shorter the survey, the more likely you'll get a good response. For an information product business, the three questions might be:

1 What were you searching for when you found us?
2 What do you want to know?
3 How hard are you finding it to get this information currently?

The most profitable information businesses will be those where survey respondents are finding it very hard to get the information you're going to provide, so question 3 is essential. Question 2 will help you shape exactly what goes into the product and will also help to identify "hyper-responsive" customers. Very broadly speaking, the more words a respondent uses in answer to question 2, the more likely they are to be interested in the product.

"We picked a price we'd feel comfortable paying ourselves."

For a product or service business, you might ask:

1 Are you searching for your own benefit or for someone else?
2 What are you looking for in this product?
3 What would be a reasonable charge for this product?

In the case of a product (as opposed to a service), question 1 might ask if they're buying it as a gift. Whatever questions you choose, the end result needs to be that you have a clear idea of what form the product or service needs to take and how much you can charge for it. Bear in mind, however, that if you're developing a novel product, your customers may not know what a reasonable price would be.

I asked Jason Fried (left), Founder and CEO of 37Signals, how he came up with his initial pricing for the web-based collaboration tool Basecamp. "We guessed. We guessed pretty well. We've made a few minor tweaks since then, but for the most part our prices have been stable for the past few years. At the end of the day we had to pick prices that we'd feel comfortable paying ourselves."

STEP BY STEP Use SurveyMonkey to create your own online survey

1 **CREATE AN ACCOUNT** Go to www.surveymonkey.com and create a free account. This allows you to create surveys with up to 100 respondents. If you find you need more, you can upgrade to a paid account. Click Create Survey and give your survey a name.

2 **ADD A DESCRIPTION** Click Add Question Here and select "Descriptive Text" as the question type. This isn't a question at all, but allows us to add informative text: in this case I'm reminding the respondent what they're going to get for completing the survey. Click Save Question.

If you want to get a good response, you'll need to offer something in return. With an information product, standard form is to give away a copy to all survey respondents (after all, this costs you next to nothing). With an online service, you would give away free access for a period of time. If you're selling a physical product, either give away a sample or, at the very least, offer a substantial discount.

3 **CHANGE QUESTION TYPE** Add another question to your survey. This time select "Multiple Choice (Only One Answer)". Add one option per line, and make sure you click Add Comment Field

if you're not certain that you can anticipate all possible answers: this gives users the option of responding in their own words. Click "Require Answer to Question" to prevent them finishing before picking an answer.

Repeat this process with the remaining questions choosing Comment/Essay Box if you want to ask an open question. Finally, add two additional text fields: one for the user's name and the other for their email address.

4 **START YOUR SURVEY** Click Collect Responses to generate an HTML link that you can embed in your website or send out in an email.

The simplest way to get survey respondents is to set up a minimal website, embed the survey link into it and advertise on Google. I describe how to create a WordPress website in Part 2; you could even use a free WordPress.com account, but I'd recommend installing it on your own domain name. This is because Google rewards sites that have been around for a while with lower advertising costs, making it cheaper when you eventually launch your site.

Find some free articles relating to your product at www.articlesbase.com to populate your home page so that Google sees your site as relevant – again reducing ad costs. Then create a Google Ad that will appear against your main keywords. Invite people to complete the survey and ensure you include the inducement in the ad.

Set a low daily budget and end the survey when you get enough responses. I ran the www.makingyourowncandles.co.uk survey until I had just under 100. As shown in step 4, above, 86% of respondents were buying for themselves – a figure that was unlikely to change much, however many responses I waited for. In the free-format responses to the question "What is the appeal of candle making?" the word "creative" came up a lot, and that will strongly influence the make-up of my product and its marketing. Finally, the most popular price was £15.

This demonstrates the power of surveys. I would have guessed that most people looking for candle-making kits would be buying them as a gift and would expect a lower price. And I'd have been wrong on both counts.

Planning your website

Your online business not only needs a website, it needs the right type of website. Before you think about design, it's essential to find a basic structure that suits your business.

Your website has a single purpose: to sell. In order to do that, however, it needs to achieve the following:

- **Capture the attention of your visitors**
- **Retain that attention**
- **Enable you to begin a long-term relationship with your visitors**
- **Convert visitors into buyers through an efficient checkout process**
- **Establish credibility**
- **Reassure potential purchasers with good contact and support features**
- **Provide best practice and legally required information**

Much of this will be achieved through the specific content of the pages in your site: good copy and reliable technology, for example. However, the structure of the site needs to be planned in advance so you can be sure you've included everything necessary. Most websites include these pages:

- **A home page** This is your front door, so get it right
- **Landing pages** The pages visitors see when they respond to your Google AdWords or email campaigns
- **About us** A page describing the company and your team. This is an opportunity to humanise your business. If you're a limited company, it's a legal requirement to include your registered address
- **Contact us** Visitors need a place to ask questions, and to see that you'll support them if they buy from you
- **Privacy policy** Visitors need to know that you will treat their details with respect. Here's the place to tell them
- **Products/services** A list or catalogue of your products and/or services. Unless there is a *very* good reason not to, you should always include prices
- **Delivery policy** Potential purchasers will want to know when they can expect their products to be delivered, whether they're physical or electronic. Same-day despatch is becoming expected for physical goods, and next-day is the bare minimum. For electronic goods, users expect instant delivery

"The core of your site will probably remain the same, but you need to be able to add and remove pages to respond to needs that arise."

Tip

Take a look at rival websites. What do you like about how they're organised? What don't you like? Also look at http://mybusiness.1and1.co.uk. This is a service that creates tailored websites for different types of business, and 1&1 (a hosting company) has researched the most popular site structure for each business type. There's nothing to lose if you sign up for a free trial – no credit card is required – and see what site structure is suggested.

USING MEDIA Typically, video and audio are used to show a product or service in use. Video is often in the form of a screencast showing software being operated; increasingly, physical products are also demonstrated. The closer you can bring the visitor to the experience of turning the product over in their hands, as in a shop, the better your chance of making a sale. Don't forget, many people are still nervous of buying online, and the more you can do to allay those fears, the better your chance of making a sale.

ORGANIC STRUCTURES Having said all this, the structure of your website shouldn't be set in stone. The core will probably remain the same, but you need to be able to add and remove pages to respond to the needs of your visitors and marketing campaigns as they arise. By creating your site in a content management system such as WordPress, you retain this flexibility.

Getting ready for business

You now know what you want to sell and how much the market will pay for it. But how much will it cost to provide? Clearly, if you can't develop the product or service for significantly less than you sell it for, you don't have a viable business. It's time to work out the details and put them together into a business plan that shows how you can make money – both for your own benefit, and to convince your bank or investors.

Your costs will depend on the type of business you're setting up. For an information product, production costs can be negligible: all it costs you is the time it takes. In most cases an information product is downloadable, but even a physical book can be published by services such as www.lulu.com at no cost to you.

For a physical product, on the other hand, costs are likely to be significant. It may be that you're buying in complete products (most likely from a wholesaler) and selling them on. In this case, the production cost is the price you pay to your supplier. If you're assembling a product from component parts, it's the cost of those parts plus any packaging. This is what we're doing with www.makingyourowncandles.co.uk (see opposite). If you've invented a product, it's the production cost plus packaging.

Now, compare the price your customers are willing to pay with the cost of production. This will give you your gross margin. What is a good margin? That depends very much on the market, but I aim for at least a 100% gross margin. While that may sound a lot, out of it needs to come the cost of doing business and, particularly, marketing.

Finally, a software service is the hardest of all to price. As with inventing a new product, the bulk of the cost in this case comes up front in development. If this is going to be expensive, you need to be very sure of your market before going ahead, since it may take some time to get that money back. Our site www.passyourtheory.co.uk was an example of this: it cost a lot to develop up front, but has remained, at its core, largely unchanged since 2005, repaying that investment many times over. Of course, had it not found a market, we would have faced a loss. The more

Expert eye

To dig underneath why people set up in business – or at least why they should – I spoke again to Larry Heiman, Senior Business Coach for E-Myth Worldwide (www.e-myth.com).

"TO TRULY CREATE A WORLD-CLASS COMPANY, IT IS essential that you have a clear business vision, or Strategic Objective, as we call it at E-Myth. Your Strategic Objective is a picture of your business when it is complete. Whether you plan on selling your business or working behind your desk every day for the rest of your life, it is imperative you know where you're going so you can guide the development of the essential processes and systems to get you there.

"Your Strategic Objective is a detailed picture of your vision of what your business will be when fully developed. It helps guide your employees, what areas of the business you focus on, your strategic goals and planning, and the overall leadership of the company.

"Your job as a business owner is to be an entrepreneurial leader. To do that, you must not only understand who you are and what you stand for, but also what it is you want to create. What is the legacy you want to leave behind? What result do you want for your employees, clients, family and community?"

Some businesses are simpler than others. Lulu lets you sell books both through your site and through Amazon with no upfront costs.

it's going to cost to bring your product to market, the more thorough your market research needs to be before you start.

BUSINESS PLAN Every business needs a business plan. Exactly what form it will take depends on whether...

1 ...you're going to need to get finance
2 ...it's a full- or part-time business
3 ...you're forming a separate company

I certainly don't believe in creating documents for their own sake and, as a rule, I suggest spending only as long as is necessary on your business plan. If you're approaching a bank for finance (or even for a bank account), you will need more detail in your plan than if it's purely for your own use. BusinessLink (www.pcpro.co.uk/links/businesslink) has a thorough guide to creating your own business plan.

By now, you should know a lot of what will go into your business plan, and creating the plan itself is simply a process of structuring that information. By going through the sections in the BusinessLink guide, you can be sure you've covered everything.

Above all else, keep your vision front and centre. Why are you setting up in business?

ACCOUNTING AND ADMIN I recommend getting your accounting sorted out before you get going. FreeAgent (www.freeagentcentral.com) is my favourite online book-keeping service and, in fact, one of my all-time favourite web applications. It makes the process of keeping the books up to date as simple as it could possibly be, and ensures that you're always aware of tax deadlines and amounts.

For organisation, I recommend Backpack (www.backpackit.com) from 37Signals. It's a flexible organisational tool that you can use in any number of ways to ensure you keep track of what you need to do, as well as forming a repository of contacts and data.

Case study
3: Defining the product

For MakingYourOwnCandles, our research indicated that we needed to aim at around £15 for our core product. We knew we had to include all the components necessary to create a batch of candles (ten in our case). We also felt it was important to use good-quality components, since our aim is to sell repeatedly to our buyers, and one aspect that differentiates us from the competition will be quality. Of course, quality is likely to cost more, so it's a challenge to get the balance right.

We began by working out what we should include. We did that by trying other kits; by looking online at what was available; and, most importantly, by making candles ourselves. We experimented with materials until we came up with the ideal combination. I then spent many hours researching suppliers until I worked out the minimum costs I'd need to pay.

We kept our core range limited: a series of kits differentiated only by their scent/dye combination, plus a refill kit and a few accessories. This means our customers will have more choice than with standard kits, but without facing the bewildering array of options offered by specialist retailers. It also means we can hope for follow-up sales of refills, accessories, oils and dyes.

A 100% margin would mean the most we could pay for the contents of our kit would be £6.50 (the retail price includes VAT, so the net price is lower). This includes the cost of packaging; in this case, a white box purchased on eBay with a home-printed sticker.

I can't emphasise enough how important it is to get the product exactly right both in terms of features and presentation. Don't short-cut the process of researching and sourcing, or you'll regret it later.

"Good quality would differentiate us from the competition. Of course, quality costs more."

Finding the money

However efficient you are, no business can be launched on a budget of zero, so you need to establish what money you need to get off the ground – and how you're going to raise it.

Your first job is to find out how much money your business needs to generate. This breaks down into finding the money to do four things, which we'll look at in turn:

1 Develop your product or service
2 Market it
3 Run your business
4 Live!

1 **DEVELOPMENT** The cost of developing your product or service will vary greatly depending on what you're selling. If you intend to go freelance in your day job, for example, there's no cost unless you'll be investing in training to polish up or widen your skills.

Information products tend to be relatively cheap to develop; usually the main cost is time, plus, if there's a physical vehicle such as a book, the production cost. For physical products, the figure you're looking for is the cost to establish a sufficient stock to get started. If you're selling a range of products, an essential part of your market research is to establish which are likely to sell best. Remember, internet shoppers have no patience: they expect delivery

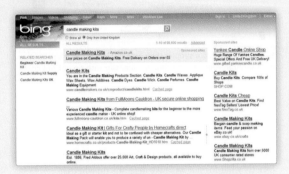

There's more to internet advertising than Google AdWords, but you should get AdWords right before moving on to Microsoft's Bing.

much you're likely to have to pay per click and what your conversion rate (the proportion of the users who click your ad who go on to buy something from you) is likely to be.

If you're paying 10p per click and expect a conversion rate of 2%, each conversion is going to cost £5. It's then a matter of deciding how many customers your marketing is likely to send to your site. If 50,000 people search on your keywords every month and you achieve a

"Many would-be entrepreneurs believe the best way to fund their business is through investors. As a rule, this should be a last resort."

within a couple of days, so you need to prepare for demand. Aim to have at least a week's stock in place.

Software development is tricky to estimate. Notoriously, it takes far longer to put together fully working software than you expect. It also suffers from the disadvantage that your costs are largely up front: you can't find out for certain whether the market is big enough to support your software until it has been developed.

2 **MARKETING** Most online businesses market themselves largely online. The beauty of systems such as Google AdWords, Yahoo! Advertising and Microsoft adCenter is that you can control very closely how much you spend and get almost instant performance feedback. When it comes to setting your budget, look at how

clickthrough (the percentage of people seeing your ad who click it) of 5%, you'll have 2,500 visitors. At a 2% conversion rate, those 2,500 visitors will produce 50 sales. These sales will have cost you £250 – so, if you wanted maximum sales in that month, this would be your advertising budget. In most cases, however, you'll want to limit your marketing spend to begin with because you'll need to optimise your campaign and can expect to improve its effectiveness by an order of magnitude within weeks. So you won't want to spend as much early on, when your campaign is less efficient.

You also need to take into account the likely cost of developing your website, and any offline marketing.

3 **RUNNING YOUR BUSINESS** You must budget for the day-to-day cost of running the business. This includes any office expenses, staff costs, stationery, hosting, software, equipment, insurance and any accountancy or other professional advice.

4 **MONEY TO LIVE ON** If this is a sideline business or you have another income, it may not be necessary to draw money out at the beginning, which will help you get started and profitable more quickly. Try to draw the absolute minimum out of the company until it's standing on its own two feet and making a steady profit.

WHERE TO GET THE MONEY Many would-be entrepreneurs believe the best way to fund their business is by attracting investors. This could range from six-figure sums from venture capitalists (a rare breed these days) right down to a few hundred quid lent by your parents.

As a rule, however, borrowing from investors of any sort should be a last resort. Commercial investors will expect part ownership – and thus partial control – as part of the deal. This is your business, and *you* should control it.

Another downside of external investment is that it can lead to long-term resentment. The business world is littered with examples of entrepreneurs giving away equity (ownership) in return for money to help start up, only for the investor to continue to have control and receive dividends years later when their input is in the distant past. This happened to me, and I know how hard it can be.

Borrowing from family is, depending on your family, usually a better idea, since they will care about your success as a person too. My recommendation is to borrow in the form of a loan that you repay at a fixed rate (including interest) over a fixed period. That way, your relative gets a good return but doesn't end up owning part of the company.

You might also consider borrowing from a bank. In the current economic climate this might be easier said than done, and will depend on a good business plan. If you're setting up a limited company, you will be asked for a personal guarantee covering the overdraft or loan if your business fails. At the other end of the scale, if you have a good credit rating you may be able to obtain an unsecured loan for a few thousand pounds with little paperwork.

The very best option is to borrow from yourself. If you're lucky enough to have savings, think about whether you can afford to ring-fence part of those to fund your business's early days. Keep a record of your investment and pay yourself back at a reasonable rate. Alternatively, many business owners make use of overdrafts and credit cards.

In the case of MakingYourOwnCandles, we estimated the cost of starting and running the business for three months (by which time we'd know if it was going to be a success or not) at £750, and this manageable amount was funded from another business we were operating.

There are many sources of funding for a new business, but if you can fund it yourself you'll avoid the need to give up part ownership or spend years tied to your initial investors.

Less is more: 37Signals

37Signals, creator of the Basecamp project-management service, has made a business out of "building less" to get its software out there earning money and gaining customers. Its book *Getting Real* (you can read it free at http://gettingreal.37signals.com/toc.php) covers this principle in depth, but here's the company's explanation in a nutshell.

"Conventional wisdom says that to beat your competitors you need to one-up them. If they have four features, you need five (or 15, or 25). If they're spending x, you need to spend xx. If they have 20, you need 30.

"This sort of one-upping Cold War mentality is a dead end. It's an expensive, defensive and paranoid way of building products. Defensive, paranoid companies can't think ahead, they can only think behind. They don't lead, they follow.

"So what to do then? The answer is less. Do less than your competitors to beat them. Solve the simple problems and leave the hairy, difficult, nasty problems to everyone else. Instead of one-upping, try one-downing. Instead of outdoing, try underdoing."

This might seem counter-intuitive, but by focusing on the central problem your software is solving, rather than simply competing on the features your competitors include, you will be able to develop it more quickly, and the end result will be simpler, more focused and, crucially, different to the competition.

37Signals has developed a range of successful online applications, all of which remain closely wedded to its original core principles.

PART 2 Building

Create the right website

FREE ULTIMATE GUIDE TO Windows 7

When you claim 3 trial issues of PC Pro today

YOUR GREAT SUBSCRIPTION DEAL

- FREE copy of the **Ultimate Guide to Windows 7**
- **3 trial issues** to start your subscription
- **Save up to 33%** on the shop price
- Receive a **disc full of software** with every issue

YOUR FREE GIFT

The Ultimate Guide to Windows 7 is packed with tips, hints and expert advice, all you need to take full advantage of Windows 7. Over 150 pages bring Windows 7 to life, detailing customisation, new concepts and new features you might have never otherwise discovered.

CALL NOW ON
0844 844 0083
or go to **www.dennismags.co.uk/pcpro**
entering offer code: P1001

PC PRO | 3 TRIAL ISSUES ORDER FORM

☐ **YES!** Please start my subscription to PC Pro with 3 trial issues and send me my FREE gift. I understand that if I'm not completely satisfied with PC Pro, I can write to cancel my subscription within my trial period and claim a FULL REFUND.
Please indicate which edition you would like ☐ **DVD edition** ☐ **CD edition**

OR ☐ **YES!** I am a current subscriber. Please extend my subscription with this offer.

Your Details

Mr/Mrs/Ms	First name
Surname	Job title
Company	
Address	
	Postcode
Daytime tel	Mobile tel
Email	Year of birth (YYYY)

Cheque or Credit/Debit Card ☐ **DVD** – £39.99 for 12 issues ☐ **CD** – £35.90 for 12 issues

❶ I enclose a cheque made payable to Dennis Publishing Ltd.

❷ Credit/Debit card: Please charge my:
☐ VISA ☐ MasterCard ☐ AMEX ☐ Switch/Maestro (Issue No. ⬚)

Card No. ⬚⬚⬚⬚ ⬚⬚⬚⬚ ⬚⬚⬚⬚ ⬚⬚⬚⬚

Start date (if applicable) ⬚⬚ ⬚⬚   Expiry date ⬚⬚ ⬚⬚

Signed   Date

❸ **Direct Debit** ☐ **DVD** – £19.99 every 6 issues ☐ **CD** – £17.95 every 6 issues

Dennis **Instruction to your Bank or Building Society to pay by Direct Debit** ⬤ **DIRECT Debit**

Please complete and send to: Freepost RLZS-ETGT-BCZR, Dennis Publishing Ltd, 800 Guillat Ave, Kent Science Park, Sittingbourne ME9 8GU
Name and full postal address of your Bank or Building Society

To the manager: Bank name	**Originator's Identification Number**
Address	7 2 4 6 8 0
Postcode	Ref no. to be completed by Dennis Publishing

Instructions to your bank or Building Society
Please pay Dennis Publishing Ltd. Direct Debits from the account detailed in this instruction subject to the safeguards assured by the Direct Debit Guarantee. I understand that this instruction may remain with Dennis Publishing Ltd and, if so, details will be passed electronically to my Bank/Building Society.

Account in the name(s) of

Branch sort code ⬚⬚ ⬚⬚ ⬚⬚

Bank/Building Society account number ⬚⬚⬚⬚⬚⬚⬚⬚

Signature(s)

Date

Banks and building societies may not accept Direct Debit instructions for some types of account

Now return your completed form to:
Freepost RLZS-ETGT-BCZR, PC Pro Subscriptions, 800 Guillat Ave, Kent Science Park, Sittingbourne ME9 8GU (No stamp required)

You will be able to view your subscription details online at www.subsinfo.co.uk

Offer code: P1001

Finding a home for your business

Choosing a base for your business used to mean selecting a shop or office for your customers to come to. An online business interacts with its customers via the internet, so the choice now is what form of online presence you need. This will serve two main purposes: to persuade the customer to buy and to act as a shopping cart to take their order.

Most businesses will also include support and background information, but the main purpose of the website is to get people to buy. A site is made up of HTML pages, along with images, sounds, videos and scripts. Broadly, you have a couple of choices when it comes to where these files are stored and served from.

The simpler option is to have your site hosted on a server owned and operated by someone else. This often means you can use your host's framework to build your internet presence very quickly with little technical knowledge. eBay is a good example of a system that not only hosts your site but also provides the tools to build it.

A number of hosts provide online site-creation tools that offer a template-driven approach to site building. The quality of these varies enormously, but the best of them (such as, from my own testing, 1and1's MyBusiness Site at www.1and1.co.uk) make it possible to create a reasonably professional, if mundane, site very quickly.

DO IT YOURSELF The second option is to rent a web server, or space on a shared server. Generally this means your development process takes longer, but you get full control. As well as being able to construct your site exactly the way you want, you can move from one host to another if you're dissatisfied with their service or, more positively, if your business grows to the extent that you need a dedicated server with higher performance.

So which option should you choose? If you sell physical goods, the quickest way to get started is to use a provider such as eBay to build a shop. You can then test the size of the market for your goods very quickly and at low cost before, perhaps, upgrading to your own independent shop.

If you sell services, information products or software then, in most cases, you will be better off renting your own space and building a site of your own, even if your shopping cart is handled by a third party. (We'll look at how this works later in this part of the book.)

Ultimately, most online businesses will benefit from being self-hosted and self-developed. A template-derived site might be fine for a plumber, but it doesn't offer the range of services, detailed editing and control that a more ambitious business will require.

Argos is one of the biggest High Street retail chains in the UK and Ireland, stocking tens of thousands of products in hundreds of stores. Its catalogue can be found in three-quarters of all homes. You might think it already had plenty of ways to communicate with and sell to customers, yet it still sees the importance of the web, not only running its own website but also using third-party outlets such as eBay. You may not be able to set up a national retail chain, but you can host a web presence just as effectively.

How to set up an eBay shop

eBay is a quick and effective way to begin selling physical products. You don't even need to market your shop – eBay does it for you. A basic eBay shop costs £14.99 per month and can be set up in minutes. But spending a little time configuring it and getting your listings right can have a huge impact on your success. Remember, you pay a listing fee whether or not your product sells, so you need all your listings to result in sales.

Here we'll walk through the process of opening up a shop with eBay. Before you start this process, there are two important hurdles to overcome. To open a Basic shop, you must have an existing eBay membership with a minimum feedback score of 10. In other words, you must have received ten feedback ratings from purchases you've made on eBay. Alternatively, you must be PayPal Verified.

Frankly, you need to be PayPal Verified in any case to be able to run any sort of business online, so I would suggest that if you're not already, you go through the process of getting verified. This is just a matter of connecting your PayPal identity to a bank account. These requirements are there to make it harder for scam artists and other undesirables to set up eBay shops and, inconvenient though it can be, it does makes sense.

YOUR PRODUCT Don't start building your shop until you have your product ready. When we set up the MakingYourOwnCandles eBay shop, we had our first sale within two hours. Online buyers expect next-day despatch at the latest, so if you haven't got an initial stock you're risking embarrassment and, worse, negative feedback.

Feedback – the ratings you're given by those who buy from you – is an incredibly important element of eBay trading.

Make sure you're very clear about the cost of making your product. Keep this in mind as you add your product listings, because eBay presents you with all sorts of opportunities to "enhance" your listings. These may help sales, but they cost money and therefore reduce your profit margin. On the plus side, listing fees are per *listing*, not per *product*: if you're selling ten products in the same listing then – assuming you sell all ten – the actual cost per product is a tenth of the total fee. Selling fees, however, accrue on top of this and are paid on each individual sale.

Follow these steps to create your eBay shop.

1   STEP INSIDE Go to www.ebay.co.uk and sign in, then point your browser to www.ebay.co.uk/shops and click "Open a Shop". (There may also be a link to this on the eBay home page, but it tends to move around quite frequently.)

2   START WITH THE BASICS You'll almost certainly want to begin with a Basic shop. "Featured" shops have lower fees to compensate for their higher monthly fee, but you need to sell a lot of products to make it worthwhile. Note, though, that Featured shops seem to appear higher than Basic shops in the product listings for any given search, all things being equal.

You also need to enter your shop name. In most cases you should be using a name that includes your search keywords, and if you intend to set up your own website, the shop name should be very similar to your domain name. In our case we've gone for MakingYourOwnCandles, which is exactly the same as our planned domain. Click Continue.

The next screen may offer you some free subscriptions to eBay products (in my case Selling Manager and Sales Reports Plus). Decide whether you want to take them up – check for small print first – and click Continue.

3   TUNE-UP TIME You'll then be asked if you want to perform a "Quick Shop Tune-up" of your nascent emporium. I suggest you take a look and decide for yourself which of the options makes sense to you. Personally, I prefer to specify the settings for my shop from the ground up. To do this, go to My eBay and select Selling. Under Shortcuts, click Manage my shop. This should bring up the "Manage my Shop" summary screen.

4   FIRST IMPRESSIONS Click Display Settings to edit the appearance of your shop. If you have a logo, make sure you include it in your design (to find out how I got my logo, and why I don't recommend you take the same route, check out www.scribbleit.co.uk/

blog/?p=229). The aim is to have your eBay shop and your future website share a similar design, even if that only really amounts to the colour scheme.

We'll look at colour choices on p54, so you might want to take a look at that when coming up with a palette. In my case, orange and yellow are considered "creative" colours, and are also reminiscent of fire, so they fitted in well with candle making.

5   SAME DIFFERENCE Click "Change to another theme" to browse through the available shop structures. Although there's a reasonable range of themes, they all tend to be much of a muchness. This is a weakness of selling on eBay, but at least everyone's in the same boat! Personally, I prefer the "classic" themes, which you can access by clicking the Easily Customisable link. I think they result in cleaner, more appealing designs which you can more easily mould to your liking. Click Save when you're done.

Choose "Edit current theme" to modify the colour scheme, some fonts, and that's about it. Choose colours from your palette and pick plain fonts (Verdana is a good choice from the limited options). Click Save Settings and then go through the other links under Shop Design to customise your shop. The most important one to sort out at this point is Product Categories. When you've finished tweaking, click the Shop Summary link to go back to the "Manage my Shop" screen.

6   OPEN FOR BUSINESS Finally, click the View My Shop link to see your shop in all its glory.

An eBay shop can never be truly "yours" in the same way as a website you design from scratch, but it's the quickest way to create a working ecommerce site. By adding your own colour scheme and logo,s you can make it look reasonably well branded.

Selling your first items on eBay

As a new eBay seller, you start at a disadvantage. eBay rewards established sellers, with high volumes and good feedback, by making it easier for their items to appear higher in the search results. At first, you're likely to be listed near the bottom of the results for any category. So what can you do about it?

Any user who searches a popular eBay category will find hundreds of results competing for attention, and the higher up the listing you are, the more views your product will have. It's therefore absolutely essential that your products appear as high as possible, but it's not obvious how you can influence that, given that you won't be a PowerSeller for some time.

Exactly how eBay ranks results is a bit of a mystery, but my observations are:

- It gives a significant boost to items that offer **free postage**. The cynical might conclude that this is because if you include postage in the price of your product, eBay makes more money, since listing fees increase according to the price of the product.

- The more you pay for your listing in terms of eBay's **optional extras**, the higher it is likely to appear relative to your other listings.

- When you're selling multiple items, **items that are already selling best** will appear above the others.

- Counterintuitively, **items with longer to go** until their listing ends will appear above those with shorter end dates. Again, it may not be a coincidence that the fees will also be higher on these items.

The 80/20 rule applies to eBay selling, just as it does to Google AdWords and many other aspects of running an online business. If you're one of the 20% of businesses that systematically analyse the impact on profitability of each of their options, you have an instant edge on your rivals – an edge that might make the difference between a viable business and a failure.

My advice is to "split-test" your listings. Wherever possible, create two listings for identical products (this works best if you're also selling in quantities). Make the listings the same except for one feature. For example, you might pay the extra fee for a subtitle on one of the listings. Run the two items simultaneously until they finish and compare the results.

First, look to see which of the two comes up higher in the rankings (you should find the subtitle gives a slight boost), then compare sales. Also compare the number of views of each product. If one of the two listings is a clear winner, your next should be based on that one, testing a new feature each time.

This may seem long-winded, but expecting instant results on eBay is a fantasy. It's only by following an analytical approach that you will develop an understanding of how to market your product effectively. Here's how to get started with your listings.

1 **BEYOND THE BASICS** Click Sell at the top of the eBay home page, then select Advanced Sell. There's a principle with systems such as eBay, Amazon and Google AdWords that you should never allow the service provider to pick your settings for you, because they're unlikely to suit your product exactly.

Type a descriptive phrase into the text box: this will help eBay find a product category. Click "Start selling", and select from the categories you're presented with. If you can't find the right category, click Browse to look through the entire category list. Click Continue.

2 **TITLES WITH IMPACT** As with a Google Ad, your title is critical. Use your research from p26 to give you a head start, and make certain your keywords are in the title. It's worth experimenting with adding "new" to the title (if your product is new) because many people still assume that all items on eBay are used.

3 **PICTURE PERFECT** Now add some pictures. The first is currently free of charge, so there's no excuse for not having a photo, and it's usually worth adding at least one more. Don't use generic shots that just convey the type of item; buyers want to see the actual product they're buying.

Make the effort to take a good photo, as it makes you look more professional. You can get perfectly acceptable results with a bog-standard digital camera: the essential part

to get right is the lighting. Natural light is often best, but you need to minimise shadows, and that often requires a couple of lamps (with "natural light" bulbs) and preferably a light tent; a small pop-up white tent used to diffuse light. If you do have a digital SLR, this is where it will pay for itself. Take all your photos in RAW mode and you can adjust the exposure and other settings without digital noise (grain) and image compression artefacts becoming visible.

4 **CLINCH THE SALE** Spend time on your descriptions. Always repeat the title of the listing at the top of the description box. You need to list, briefly, what you're offering and, if you have a unique selling point, say what that is. eBay buyers have very short attention spans, so you must clinch the sale early – in this respect, less is more. ➜

Attractive photos of your product are well worth the effort, as they'll make all the difference when buyers are choosing between numerous listings. If any objects appear in the photo that are not part of what you're selling, make sure this is clearly stated in the description, even if you think it's obvious.

Basic | Self Hosting

Select pictures for upload   Try the

(First picture is free. Each additional picture is £0.12.)Add up to 12 pictures.

Browse..   Recommended size: Between 1000 and 1600 pixels on the longer side

	Pictures	Status
1	teacup.jpg	Pending
2	candlemakingsamplekit.jpg	Pending

Copied 0 / Pending 2 / Available 10

Select optional picture upgrades

ⓘ Good news! Gallery Picture is free. Add a picture and we will show your item to buyers in se

3

Add pictures   Remove all pictures

1   2

« » 🗑   « » 🗑

ⓘ Good news! Gallery Picture is free. Add a picture and we'll show your item to buyers in search re

★ **Describe the item you're selling**   Add or remove options | Get help

Standard | HTML

Arial   ▼   10 ▼   A▾   B I U   ≣ ≣ ≣   ≔ ≔   ≖ ≖   ✓ Check spel

candle. This is the ideal way to have a go at candle making at very low expens

Candle making offers you the enjoyment both of making the candles and

4

→ You can just use the standard editor for most purposes, but if you know a little HTML you can add tags to include other media for no extra fee. This is well worth doing to enhance your listing with elements such as your logo and extra photos.

5 PRICING OPTIONS In most cases you'll want to list your items as "Buy it Now" purchases. The advantage of this to the buyer is that they don't have to wait until the end of the auction to know they've secured the item – it's more like buying from a shop. You can experiment with the auction option once you make a success of "Buy it Now". Also enter how many you want to sell: if you have multiples of the same product, entering the quantity here cuts down on your listing fees and adds to your credibility as a retailer rather than a private seller.

As a new eBay shop-owner you may be limited to accepting only PayPal, but in any case PayPal should always be an option. If you have the ability to accept cheques as well, you need to decide whether the hassle of doing so outweighs the extra sales you might generate; few retailers accept cheques these days, but some eBayers prefer them to PayPal.

Now for the important question of postage. eBay likes items with free post and packing, so your first split test should be to see if you can make more money increasing the price to include it (thus making p&p "free") or selling at a lower price plus p&p (and coming further down the results).

As an example, my first split test resulted in the item with free p&p appearing 34 places above the identical item with additional postage. That's an amazing result given that there were only 98 items in the list overall, and it put the free p&p version of my item on the front page.

At the bottom of the page you'll see "Your fees so far": remember these eat into your profit. Click Continue.

6 FEATURE PRESENTATION You'll see a number of options under the section "Make your listing stand out". Most of these will have a positive impact on sales, although it may be minor. This is an area you should test, beginning with the cheapest option. Featured Plus is expensive and guarantees only that you'll appear at the top of the search page *that you'd normally appear on*. In other words, if you would otherwise appear halfway down page 3 of the results, paying for Featured Plus would make you appear at the top of page 3.

If you select Featured First, you stand a chance of appearing at the top of the first page – depending, presumably, on how many others are also paying for this. These very expensive options should be experimented with only once you've nailed down your pricing and presentation.

Check out the listing preview to ensure it looks how you want it to. Make sure you review your fees and, crucially, note the Final Value Fee. The Listing Fee is paid once, no matter how many items you're selling within the same listing; the Final Value Fee is paid per sale. Be certain you can make a profit after these are taken into account.

Once finished, don't forget to click "Save this listing as a template" so that you can base other product listings on it. Click "List your item". Give it a few minutes and see where it appears when you search for it.

"Expecting instant results is a fantasy. With an analytical approach, you will develop an understanding of how to market your product."

Content management systems

When it comes to setting up your own website, on your own domain, just as you want it, you'll need somewhere to start. A content management system (CMS) offers an alternative to doing it all from scratch. For our purposes, a CMS is a ready-made system that enables you to create and edit a website without needing to code it by hand. Once installed on your web server, a CMS can be used to set up and edit the appearance, content and capabilities of your site through a browser-based user interface.

In short, content management systems are:

 Quick to get up and running, so you can create a fully working customised site in a few hours

Extendable through plug-ins, making it possible to incorporate additional functionality, often free

Reliable and continually updated, if you choose one of the big players

On the other hand, CMSes are not without their disadvantages. If your site is likely to be *very* simple, the benefits of using a CMS may be outweighed by the bother of installing one. If you're more ambitious, bear in mind that you're limited to the CMS's functionality (albeit extended through plug-ins), and if you

need something specific you might find it doesn't exist. You could create a new plug-in yourself, or hire someone to do so, but this isn't a process for the faint-hearted.

There is one further option, which is to create your site from scratch (or hire a web developer to do it) and incorporate one of the plethora of "micro-CMSes" into it. In this case, the web developer incorporates special fields into the editable pages and the micro-CMS provides an interface for you to update and add content to without needing to edit the HTML itself. A good example is Perch (www.grabaperch.com) from UK design agency edgeofmyseat.com.

TAKE YOUR PICK The three leading players in affordable content management are

WordPress, Joomla and Drupal. All three are open source, free and written in PHP, which means they'll work with most web hosts. If you're looking for the most fully featured CMS with the best support for multiple authors and detailed user management, choose between Drupal and Joomla (with Drupal edging it for most purposes in my view), but as our task is to create an everyday business website, WordPress is by far the best choice.

WordPress is simpler to install and, especially, to get working. It has a wide range of plugins available that extend its functionality (such as shopping carts), and there are thousands of themes from various developers, many free, to change its look and feel. As these are essentially CSS, they can be amended to give you exactly the front end you want.

Joomla is ideal for small company websites where collaboration is part of the functionality on offer. For our example project, however, it's slightly more complex than necessary.

Content management systems are the basis of all kinds of websites, from simple blogs to fully featured commercial sites, enabling them to be set up quickly and at low cost and maintained easily.

Building a website from scratch

If you're selling physical products, hosting your shop on eBay or using a content management system with a shopping cart plugin or an external cart may do the job. But for an online service, an information product or any technology-related business, you may want or need to create a site of your own.

And regardless of the nature of your business, you may simply prefer the idea of getting exactly what you want. The main downsides of creating a website from scratch are the time it takes and, if you outsource the actual coding of the site, the cost. There's also a greater chance of bugs, since both eBay's framework and the leading content management systems are tried and tested, while your own site won't have been through this process yet.

We've already explained how CMSes offer a halfway house between a ready-made web presence and a completely new site. Even if you think you need a bespoke website, there's often a benefit in getting an initial web presence together using WordPress before migrating it to your own platform, either at the official launch or afterwards. By quickly creating a WordPress site and populating it with articles ahead of launching your product or service, you can be picking up subscribers to use for your initial marketing. Google AdWords will also be cheaper, because your site is already established.

BASIC PRINCIPLES Any modern website must obey the principle of separating content, presentation and interactivity. What this means in practice is that HTML is used purely to "mark up" the meaning and relative importance of your content (the "semantics"), not control exactly how it appears onscreen. The appearance of the website is determined by cascading style sheets (CSS) files that are also stored on your server and imported into the HTML when it's loaded into the user's browser window. Interactivity is provided by external JavaScript or Flash files.

In other words, the HTML of your site shouldn't contain any "presentational" markups, such as <font> tags or old favourites like <b> (bold) . When you want to emphasise that one piece of text is more important, you give it a heading tag, such as <h1>, or use <strong> or <em> (emphasis) to indicate that it should have a special style. None of these dictates how the text will look: that's the job of your CSS, which will specify what the browser should do to the content when it comes across each of these tags.

There are a number of benefits to this approach:

- You can change the look of the entire site by editing a single CSS file (often known as a 'theme') rather than having to edit every HTML page

Editing "raw" HTML in a programmer's editor such as PSPad requires confident coding skills.

Visual editors such as Adobe Dreamweaver make advanced sites easier to construct, but there are a lot of tools to learn.

- Google finds it much easier to index a site created using these principles, as the HTML is so much cleaner and easy to understand
- For the same reason, screen readers and other "assistive technologies" work better with pages like this, helping to ensure users with disabilities can access your site – good for business, and a legal requirement
- Your site can easily be adapted for mobile devices: the HTML stays the same but a different CSS file can be specified for these devices and, indeed, for printers
- Once your CSS or JavaScript file has been downloaded into the user's internet cache (and this should only need to happen once), your pages will load much more quickly compared to having the same style information repeated on every page in the HTML
- If you wish, you can work on the design while a web developer works on the programming, or vice versa. The designer will be primarily working with the CSS and the programmer with HTML, PHP or whatever

HTML is the original language of the world wide web. Today it's complemented by cascading style sheets (CSS), enabling the content of a website to be stored independently of its appearance – a key principle of modern web design.

The current standard for HTML is XHTML 1.0, and you should insist on your site being compliant with the "strict" form of that standard. Despite how it might sound, this isn't onerous at all, and it will help make sure that when new standards come out, the minimum of extra work needs to be done. The current standard for CSS is CSS2, which is supported well on all modern browsers. The main reason to comply with standards is simply to ensure the maximum number of users can see your pages as you intended them.

Use JavaScript for simple interactivity. For example, if you want to add an email contact form you could use JavaScript to check that the user has completed all the fields. Don't use it for adding jaunty animations; they weren't a good idea even in the 1990s.

For more sophisticated interactivity, use the Flash SWF format. This doesn't mean you have to buy Adobe's Flash authoring application, since there are a number of low-cost tools that will output to Flash at much lower cost and are easier to use. Examples include SWiSH Max2 (www.swishzone.com) for general use, SWiSH miniMax2 for simpler animations, and Mix-FX (www.mix-fx.com) for Flash buttons and banners. Do keep in mind that iPhone users, for example, can't currently see Flash content, so you may want to ensure that parts of your site will work without Flash.

TOOLS FOR THE JOB If you decide to develop your site yourself, you'll need an HTML/programmer's text editor and/or a visual web design package. The main visual tools are Adobe Dreamweaver CS4 (www.adobe.com/products/dreamweaver) and Microsoft Expression Web 3 (www.microsoft.com/expression/products/Web_Overview.aspx).

Which you choose will probably depend on which of the two companies you tend to buy from; both are quite complex, and it might be overkill to install one of these and learn to use it just to create a straightforward online shop front.

If you really want to understand how to build a website – or you want to save yourself a couple of hundred quid – you should use an HTML editor. My current favourite for general web work is PSPad (www.pspad.com/en) which, as well as being fully featured, is entirely free. If you feel like treating yourself, UltraEdit (www.ultraedit.com) is a low-cost commercial text editor that's not only fully featured but also under constant development.

You'll no doubt want to include pictures on your site, and these will need preparing in the required size and format. The open-source image editor The Gimp (www.gimp.org) has plenty of features but is also devilishly idiosyncratic and is likely to drive you nuts. I recommend investing in a copy of Adobe Photoshop Elements (www.adobe.com/products/photoshopelwin), which will give you all the power you're likely to need. Alternatives include Corel Paint Shop Pro Photo (www.corel.com/psp) and the free Serif PhotoPlus SE (www.freeserifsoftware.com). If you intend to add video to your site, perhaps to demonstrate your product, you might as well buy the Photoshop Elements/Premiere Elements bundle, which includes Adobe's excellent budget video editor.

You can build a static website – one that has no server-generated elements – on your PC without installing anything else. Create your HTML, CSS and JavaScript files and copy them into a folder on your hard disk; then simply double-click the HTML to launch your browser.

Introduction to HTML

The web becomes ever more sophisticated, yet the underlying standards and technologies have remained largely unchanged for the past ten years. Armed with a free text editor, an understanding of the principles and a dictionary of tags and rules, you can create an entire website from scratch – and even though we don't recommend you do that, it's useful to know what underpins your site. Stand by for a whistle-stop tour.

HTML (short for "hypertext markup language") is used to deliver the content of a web page. Although it was originally also used to dictate how the page should look, that's now the role of CSS (cascading style sheets). Both HTML and CSS code are stored in ordinary plain text files on the web server. When you access a web page by typing its address into a web browser such as Internet Explorer, Firefox or Safari, the browser reads these files and displays the page on your screen accordingly.

HTML works by providing a library of predefined tag pairs that you use to "mark up" your content. These tags are always written in lower case, with angle brackets, and must always be "closed": that is, an opening tag must be followed eventually by a closing tag. Here's an example:

```
<p>This is a paragraph.</p>
```

`<p>` is the paragraph tag, and tells the browser that the text that follows is a new paragraph. When the browser sees the closing tag `</p>` it knows it's the end of the paragraph.

The heading tags `<h1>`, `<h2>`, `<h3>` and so on are used to mark up headings. There should only be one `<h1>` on each page, and generally speaking fewer `<h2>` tags than `<h3>` and so on. For example:

```
<h1>This is the main heading of this page</h1>
<p>This is the first paragraph.</p>
<p>This is the second paragraph.</p>
<h2>This is a second-level heading</h2>
<p>And this is the next paragraph.</p>
```

These tags organise your content "semantically": that is, meaningfully. Headings create hierarchy, telling us which parts are important. That's useful for search engines such as Google, because if you're looking for "candle making", a site that has "Making candles" as a headline is more likely to be relevant than one that just mentions it within a paragraph.

In the screenshot below left, the browser has formatted the headings for us. This is what happens when no custom formatting is specified. Although we can see the hierarchy, it would be better to define exactly how we want the tags to appear, and we can use CSS to do this.

HIDDEN STRUCTURE You can see the markup behind any web page by going to it in your browser and viewing the "source code": in Internet Explorer, choose Source from the View menu; in Firefox, Page Source; in Safari, View Source.

The first two lines give the browser information about the website's format. Then the entire page is

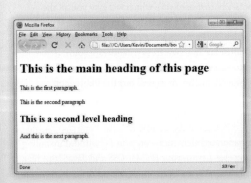

How our basic HTML example appears with no CSS styling.

With CSS, we can dictate exactly how each tag affects the appearance.

Top 10 HTML tags

Tag	Description	Usage
<h1>, <h2> etc	Used to mark up headings, with <h1> being the top-level heading	<h1>Top-level heading</h1>
<p>	Paragraph	<p>This is a paragraph.</p>
<strong>	Indicates that text is important. By default, **bold** (use instead of <b>)	<p>This is <strong>important</strong></p>
<em>	Indicates that text is emphasised. By default, italic (use instead of <i>)	<p>This is <em>emphasised</em></p>
<div>	Divides content into blocks that can be laid out by CSS code	<div id="maincontent"><!-- My content ---></div>
<a>	Used to insert hyperlinks; the href attribute contains the link itself	<a href="http://www.pcpro.co.uk">PC Pro</a>
<img>	Used to insert pictures; the src attribute specifies the picture file name*	<img src= "http://www.pcpro.co.uk/logo.jpg" />
<ul>, <ol> <li>	Lists: <ul> is unordered (bullet points), <ol> is ordered (numbered list)†	<!-- A list --><ul><li>Item 1</li><li>Item 2</li></ul>
<blockquote>	Indicates quoted text. Might be used when showing a customer comment	<blockquote>Your site is excellent!</blockquote>
<span>	Used to style text within a paragraph, such as a large initial letter (drop cap)	<p><span>D</span>rop capitals look good</p>

*This is a single tag, not a pair, since it has no contents. Note the / at the end to satisfy the requirement for tags to be closed; this tag is "self-closing".
† Unordered lists are often used for web page navigation links, using CSS rules to omit the bullet symbols and line breaks that would normally apply.

```
<?xml version="1.0" encoding="utf-8"?>
<!DOCTYPE html PUBLIC "-//W3C//DTD XHTML 1.1//EN" "http://www.w3.org/TR/xhtml1
<html xmlns="http://www.w3.org/1999/xhtml" xml:lang="cs" lang="cs">
  <head>
    <meta http-equiv="content-type" content="text/html; charset=utf-8" />
    <link href="styles.css" rel="stylesheet" type="text/css">
    <title>My First Web page</title>
  </head>
  <body>
    <h1>This is the main heading of this page</h1>
    <div id="main">
      <h2>Content Area</h2>
      <p class="standout">This is the first paragraph.</p>
      <p>This is the second paragraph</p>
    </div>
    <div id="sidebar">
      <h2>This is a second level heading</h2>
      <p class="standout">And this is the next paragraph.</p>
    </div>
  </body>
</html>
```

This is the HTML for our example web page. You can examine the code of any site using the View, Source command in your browser.

contained within the <html></html> tag pair, which itself has two sections: <head> and <body>. The head contains the <title> tag, which shows the text that will appear in the browser's title bar, and <meta> tags, which we'll cover later.

The visible part of a web page is contained in the <body> tag. When you're checking out the source of a web page, this is the bit to concentrate on, and the key thing to remember is that if you can make sense of it fairly easily, Google's search technology will also be able to read it.

LOOK AND FEEL CSS is used to tell the browser how to render each tag. Your CSS is normally contained in a separate text file that's linked to your HTML by the line:

```
<link href="styles.css" rel="stylesheet"
type="text/css">
```

where you'd replace "styles.css" with the name of your CSS file. The file itself contains a series of rules that are used to apply styling to parts of the HTML page. For example:

```
p {
    font-family: tahoma, arial, helvetica,sans-
      serif;
    font-size: 1em;
    color:darkblue;
}

h1 {
    font-family: georgia, "times new roman",
      times, serif;
    font-size: 2em;
    color:red;
    border-bottom: 2px solid black;
}
```

These rules apply to all <p> and <h1> tags. Notice how curly brackets contain all the styles you're applying to a given "class". When a browser reads this CSS in conjunction with our HTML, it changes our rudimentary page to look like the example at the bottom right of p48. Hardly a work of art, but you can see how it goes further than the default version.

CSS allows you to target specific parts of the page in two main ways: using "class selectors" and "id selectors". A class selector might look like this:

```
p.standout {
    color: darkgreen;
}
```

This applies to paragraphs in a class called "standout", so you would mark up the paragraphs you want to style like this:

```
<p class= "standout">The paragraph content
  here.</p>                              →
```

CSS rules

The CSS rules are fairly self-explanatory (you'll find plenty of places online to look them up), and each comprises two parts: the rule name and the parameters. The font-family rule specifies a series of fonts, with the one you want to use on the left, the others being backups in case that font is not installed on the user's computer. The border-bottom rule is a specific composite rule; you can put its parameters in any order. The font-size can be given in points, pixels or ems. Ems refers to the width of the letter "m" in the font, and it's relative, so if the user increases the zoom factor in their browser, all rules that use ems will resize in proportion.

Top 10 CSS rules

Rule	Description	Usage
font-family	Specifies the font(s) to use for a tag, in order of preference; "serif" and "sans-serif" are generic	font-family: tahoma, helvetica,sans-serif;
font-size	In pt (points), px (pixels), % (of 1em) or em. Ems ensures proportional zoom in all browsers	font-size: 1em;
color	Specifies text colour using either a standard colour name or a hexadecimal RGB number	color:red; color:#ff0000;
background-color	Specifies the background colour for the tag	background-color: green; background-color: #00ff00;
padding, margin	Add empty space. Imagine a photo on a table: padding is the width of its border, margin is the space between the photo and table edge	padding: 10px 20px 30px 40px; /*10 pixels at the top, 20 on the right, 30 at the bottom and 40 on the left*/
text-align	Specifies alignment of text: left, centre or right	text-align:center;
width, height	Used with <div>s to specify block dimensions	width: 600px; height: auto;
background-image	Normally sets an image behind a <div>. Use with background-repeat, background-position to govern where the image goes and if it tiles	background-image:url("../images/logo.jpg"); background-repeat: no-repeat; background-position: top center;
float	Specifies how a <div> is placed on the page	float:right;
display	Specifies whether the item should be broken up by line feeds (as with a paragraph) or not	display:inline;

* Used with a <li> tag, makes each list item appear to the right of the last rather than beneath it.

→ An ID selector might look like this:

```
#standout {
    color:darkgreen;
}
```

In this case only one tag per page may be named "standout":

```
<p id= "standout">The paragraph content is here.</p>
```

CSS can also be used for layout. You may see the HTML

<table> element used for layout purposes, but this should be avoided unless you're actually designing a table. The <div> tag should be used to organise content into blocks; with CSS you can place the <div>s wherever you want on the page.

The screenshot on the previous page shows how the HTML of our page might look. Below left you can see some of the CSS we might use to style it, and below right you can see how this creates a two-column layout. Note that our HTML has barely changed; all the layout and formatting is handled by the CSS file, which could be linked from many HTML pages. One of the benefits of this is that by changing just the CSS we can change the look of our entire site.

```
h1{
    font-family: georgia, "times new roman", times, serif;
    font-size: 2em;
    color:red;
    border-bottom: 2px solid black;
}
h2 {
    font-family: tahoma, arial, helvetica,sans-serif;
    font-size: 1.5em;
}

p.standout {
    color: darkgreen;
}

#main {
    float:left;
    padding-right:20px;
    border-right:1px solid lightGrey;
}

#sidebar {
    float:right;
```

Once your HTML is properly marked up, you can use CSS (left) to style it and lay it out on the page exactly as you want it (above).

Firewall | VPN | QoS | **1000** Mbps | 3G Data | Wi-Fi PROTECTED SETUP

Vigor 2820 Series
The Ultimate ADSL Firewall/Router

- ADSL/ADSL2+ and Broadband Router
- 3G (Cellular) Modem & phone support
- Dual-WAN ports for ADSL, cable modem or both
- 802.11n Draft 2.0 Wireless (WiFi Certified)
- Comprehensive and robust stateful Firewall
- Twin VoIP ports with PSTN passthrough
- Content Filtering (by keyword or data type)
- NAS Facility (requires USB memory key) - New!

- Ethernet wired and WiFi Virtual LAN
- Rack Mountable (Optional kit)
- Configurable QoS (traffic prioritisation)
- VPN Dial-in/dial-out with VPN co-processor
- Gigabit LAN Port for server connectivity
- USB Port for Printer or 3G Cellular Modem
- Highly configurable and easy to monitor
- See Web site for full product details

Vigor120	Vigor2710 Series	VigorSwitch Series	Vigor2950 Series	Vigor3300V
ADSL Ethernet Modem	SoHo ADSL Router	PoE or Gigabit Ethernet	Dual WAN Security Firewall	Enterprise Multiservice Security Router

• True ADSL Ethernet Modem	• ADSL2+ SoHo Router	• Power-over-Ethernet (PoE)	• High Performance (90Mb/s)	• 4 Load-Balanced WAN Ports
• ADSL Parameters pre-set for UK	• 802.11n WiFi	• Gigabit & SFP Connectivity	• Dual Ethernet WAN Ports for load balancing or WAN backup	• Robust firewall
• ADSL, ADSL2, ADSL2+ Support	• CSM (Content Security Management)	• Layer 2 fully managed	• VPN Trunking	• 802.1q VLAN
• Ideal for load-balancing routers	• USB Storage (NAS)	• Stackable	• 5-port Gigabit LAN with VLAN	• Web filter (keyword/categoric)
	• VoIP capability with 2 phone ports	• SNMP Management	• Robust firewall & QoS	• Up to 8 FXO/FXS VoIP ports
	• QoS for high VoIP quality	• VLAN and 802.1q	• CSM (Content Security Management)	• QoS for high VoIP Quality
		• See web site for range	• 200 High Performance VPN tunnels	• Configurable DMZ ports
				• 200 VPN tunnels

PC PRO 2007 WIRELESS ROUTER AWARD | PC PRO 2008 WIRELESS ROUTER AWARD | PC PRO 2009 WIRELESS ROUTER AWARD

Dray Tek
www.draytek.co.uk

E&OE. All specifications subject to change. Please check web site for current model specifications.

Creating a basic web page using CSS and XHTML

Having at least a basic understanding of how a web page is put together will pay dividends, even if you only plan to sell through eBay. That's because eBay lets you include HTML tags in both your shop layout and your item description. If you know how, you can add links, pictures and other media free of charge.

On the other hand, if you do intend to create your own site using a content management system such as WordPress, understanding basic HTML tags and CSS means you can customise its look and feel.

Let's get started. I'm using PSPad (www.pspad.com/en), so you'll need to download it to follow along, but there are lots of other text editors suited to HTML.

1 **TIME TO BE STRICT** Go to File > New File and, in the dialog box that appears, click the Use Template tab. Scroll down the list to find XHTML, click the "+" to expand the sub-options, and select "XHTML 1.0 Strict utf-8". XHTML 1.0 is the latest stable standard for HTML, and there's no point, as far as I'm concerned, in creating web pages for anything other than the Strict version of the standard. Don't worry, this just means the bad habits that some earlier web designers picked up (and, in many cases, still use) are not tolerated, which helps to ensure your pages look right in every user's browser.

2 **DRAWING A BLANK** You'll end up with a blank XHTML page like the screen below. Section A informs the browser what to expect in terms of standards and character encoding. Give it no further thought. Section B is the Header section, which contains "meta" data to inform search engines and browsers about the content of the page itself. The information between the `<title>` and `</title>` tags will appear in the title bar of the user's browser window and also in Google searches, so it's critical to get this right – and to include your keywords in it.

Section C, between the `<body>` and `</body>` tags, contains the actual content of the page, and that's where we'll focus our energy for now.

3 **CONTENT IS KING** Rule number one is "content before style". Your first job, therefore, is to get the content in place. All you need to worry about at this time is how to organise the content, both across pages and also within the page. Use heading

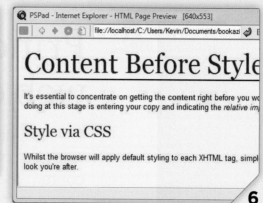

tags (<h1>, <h2> and so on, as discussed on pp48-50) to mark up your headings in order of importance. There should only be one <h1> per page, with the next most important headings using the <h2> tags and so on.

Wrap paragraphs in the <p> tag: that is, put <p> before each paragraph's text and </p> after. If you want to make a word or phrase stand out, use the <strong> or <em> tags. By default, the browser will render text marked up with the <strong> tag in bold and <em> as italic, but the benefit of using these tags rather than the old-fashioned <b> and <i> tags is that, using CSS, <strong> can be formatted however you like; for example, in red rather than bold. While it is possible to redefine the <b> tag in CSS, it would be misleading because <b> clearly stands for "bold".

4 **PREVIEW TIME** Press F10 in PSPad to see a preview of your page. As you can see, it's pretty boring, but the document structure is very clear: bear in mind that this is how the page appears to Google's robots, which don't see your fancy formatting. But users do, so let's add some CSS.

Begin by typing the following into the <head> section (for example, immediately before </head>):

```
<link rel="stylesheet" type="text/css" media=
  "all" href="styles.css" />
```

This creates a link to a CSS file that we'll create in a moment. You can include CSS within the HTML page, but unless this page is to be styled differently to the rest of the site, it's much better to store your CSS externally; it can then be applied to every other page just by including the link.

In PSPad, go to File > New File and select CSS/Default. Save it immediately as "styles.css". CSS works by defining rules for XHTML tags. Each rule is made up of one or more properties contained within a set of curly brackets.

5 **BETTER TEXT** Let's begin by changing the default text style to something nicer than Times

New Roman. Looking at the first rule, "body" is the selector – the part of the rule that specifies which tags or elements the rule is going to apply to. In this case, our rule will apply to all content between the <body> tags: in other words, all the content (see 'Body form', right). To change the font we add a property name and property value: in this case, "font-family" is the name, and the list of fonts that follows it is the value. What we're doing here is specifying a preferred order for our fonts. If the browser finds MS Trebuchet, it will use it; otherwise it works its way along the list until it finds one that's available. The final one is the generic system font.

We then specify a font size using "em" as the unit. You could use points or pixels, but ems are usually preferable because they're a relative unit. Technically, one em is the default font size, so we're setting the font to be slightly smaller than this. The benefit of this is that if the user uses the Zoom function in an older web browser, this will cause all text defined in ems to increase in size proportionately, whereas fixing the size in points or pixels would mean the Zoom function didn't affect the text. Finally, we set a background colour using one of the standard colour names (you can find them at www. w3schools.com/css/css_colornames.asp).

We now need to specify rules for the headings. The first selector ("h1,h2") defines rules that apply to both the <h1> and <h2> sections of your XHTML. We then have individual selectors to set further rules that will differ between <h1> and <h2>. In this case <h1>, along with being bigger, also has an underline (as seen in the results, step 6).

Finally, we specify that we want all <strong> text to be shown in dark blue.

6 **THE RESULTS** Press F10 to preview your work. It's still primitive so far, but it's a big improvement on the original for very little work. The important thing to remember is that we've altered the look of the page without touching the XHTML. We could just as easily give it a completely different look and feel (try it!) just by changing the CSS file. And this file can be used right across our site.

Body form

You might wonder why we bother with the <body> tag when the text within our page is all contained within <p> tags anyway. The reason is that by using <body>, we're specifying a default that will apply to every tag within the body section of the page unless it's overridden by another more specific tag. Until we write a rule for the <p> tag, therefore, the text takes on the appearance defined in the <body> rule. If we wanted to add a list using the <li> (list item) tag, it would also take on the applicable properties set in the body rule unless we overrode it. So by specifying our default rules using <body>, a lot of repetition is avoided and the need to create rules for every tag is eliminated.

Principles of good web design

The likes of WordPress and Joomla can take much of the hard work out of creating a website, but whether you're using a content management system, a more basic template or building your site from scratch, you need to understand the basics of design if you want to make a good impression.

Design students will have heard of the "Golden Ratio". This number (1.61803399 or thereabouts) describes how the size of the elements of a building, a work of art or, in our case, a web page should relate to each other to give a pleasing effect. If I decide the area of my web page that will be occupied by my copy (text) is going to be the biggest – as it usually should be – then I should make it 1.62 times wider than the smaller column containing my navigation and logo.

There are various theories to support the Golden Ratio, but why not just get on and use it? In fact, I recommend an even simpler approach, which in turn will be familiar to photographers: the Rule of Thirds. If you have one column 1.62 times wider than the other, the smaller column occupies roughly one third of the overall width and the bigger one two thirds. So you can get almost exactly the same effect by dividing your page into three.

Whichever way you achieve it, balance is one of the key aspects of design that separates the professional site from the amateur.

WHITE SPACE One of the other defining elements of a professional design is the active use of white space. White space is any area that doesn't contain text or graphics. It doesn't have to be white, just empty. Amateurs cram their websites full of text and images, all jostling together. Designers use white space to separate elements and, in designer-speak, "give them room to breathe". Take a look at just about any professional website, even the notoriously information-rich Amazon, and you'll see how white space is used. It makes a page look more pleasing and, if you want a more mercenary justification, helps draw the user's eye to the parts you want them to pay attention to.

"Whichever way you achieve it, balance is one of the key aspects of design that separates the professional from the amateur."

Windows fonts / Mac fonts / Font family	
Normal style	**Bold style**
Arial, Arial, Helvetica, *sans-serif*	**Arial**, Arial, Helvetica, *sans-serif*
Arial Black, Arial Black, Gadget, *sans-serif*	**Arial Black, Arial Black, Gadget, *sans-serif***
Comic Sans MS, Comic Sans MS[5], *cursive*	**Comic Sans MS, Comic Sans MS[5], *cursive***
Courier New, Courier New, Courier[6], *monospace*	**Courier New, Courier New, Courier[6], *monospace***
Georgia[1], Georgia, *serif*	**Georgia[1], Georgia, *serif***
Impact, Impact[5], Charcoal[6], *sans-serif*	**Impact, Impact[5], Charcoal[6], *sans-serif***
Lucida Console, Monaco[5], *monospace*	**Lucida Console, Monaco[5], *monospace***

Only certain fonts are normally used for text on web pages, since others aren't likely to exist on the majority of computers.

The BBC's website is a perfect example of the Rule of Thirds. Each page is divided into three vertical columns, with some elements spanning two columns to give an approximate Golden Ratio of two-thirds to one-third. The colour scheme is basically analogous (using tints of one colour for a calm feel), but some elements are colour-coded with other hues; a consistent medium level of saturation (how vivid the colours are) helps to tie everything together.

An immediate way to add white space to a typical web page is to increase the line height to at least 1.5 times its standard setting (150%); I prefer a setting of 175%.

COLOUR The key to coming up with a colour scheme is to begin with a base colour. If you have a logo, the base colour can be taken from the dominant colour in it. If you need inspiration, I suggest browsing the web for colours you like. Bear in mind that each colour invokes a different emotion in the user, so take care before making your final choice. You can find out more about this at www.color-wheel-pro.com/color-meaning.html. If you aim to sell globally, you may need to consider the cultural implications of your colours.

Once you've picked a base colour, find out its colour value. This is usually given in hexadecimal notation, where the numbers 0 to 9 have their usual meaning and the letters "a" to "f" then take you up to 15. You don't need to worry about this as long as you remember that the first two figures represent red, the second pair green, and the final pair blue. The higher the number (00 being the lowest, ff the highest and 88 somewhere in between), the more red, green or blue is in the final colour. By mixing these, you can create any colour visible to the human eye; in fact, that's exactly how your computer screen displays its range of colours.

COLOUR SCHEMES One way of representing the full gamut of colours is in the form of a colour wheel. Whether two colours work together can be seen from their positions: opposite colours are "complementary", so they create maximum contrast and balance when used together, while colours close to each other are "analogous", giving a more laid-back feel.

You can use Adobe's free online tool, kuler (http://kuler.adobe.com), to generate a colour scheme, as seen overleaf. All you need to use this is an Adobe account, which is free to create if you don't already have one. Once you've signed in, select Mykuler and create a new scheme. The middle colour in the row is defined as the Base Color. Below, the numbers represent colour values described in various ways. If you have a colour in mind, enter its values into one of the spaces provided, then click Set as Base.

Kuler allows you to apply any one of a series of rules to generate a fresh colour palette. If you're following along in Kuler right now, the range you're probably seeing is Analogous, which picks a series of colours all next to each other on the wheel. The effect is of a subtle change from left to right. Experiment by switching rules until you get a palette you like: it saves you the hassle of working out which colours go together. ➜

Building on the traditional colour wheel method, Adobe's Kuler leaves you no excuse for creating a colour scheme that doesn't work.

→ While these are called "rules", they're just a guide. If you're a non-designer, I suggest you base your design on a "monochromatic" or "shades" colour scheme, then add a complementary colour to brighten it up. One rule of thumb is that the more photographs (or other colourful images) you use, the fewer colours you should have in your design.

Most sites use white for their main content area and black for their body text, so the colours you've chosen will most often be used for the space outside the content area (the canvas or background) and for graphical elements. Some sites swap this and use black for content with white text (like kuler) and that's fine: the key is to get legible contrast between the content and the background.

FONTS Rule number one: don't use Comic Sans. Ever. No, really. Back when desktop publishing began, suddenly the local vicar had access to, oh, tens of fonts, and felt the need to use them all. On every page. Far too many websites adopt the same approach and end up as an amateurish mess. Things can only get worse if you choose fonts such as Comic Sans that aren't designed according to any conventional principles, and therefore convey no sense of authority or professionalism and, in large amounts, are painful to read.

So, rule number two: limit the number of fonts you use. I suggest between no more than three per page. You can get away with one, but most well-designed sites use two or three. Generally speaking, you'll use one font for all your headings and one for your body copy (paragraphs). Any additional fonts will be for specific purposes.

Fonts – or, strictly speaking, the typefaces that they embody – come in three kinds: serif, sans serif and decorative. Decorative fonts, such as THIS and *this*, should be used very sparingly, if at all. Serifs are the little hooks on the ends of letters such as these; typefaces that lack them, like this, are sans serif. Serif faces include **Times New Roman** and **Georgia**, the latter being rightly popular on the web because it's easy to read and looks good at a range of sizes. Sans serifs include **Arial** and **Verdana**.

Print designers can choose from thousands of typefaces, but when a user visits your web page they'll only see the fonts you've specified if those fonts are already installed on their computer. A list of the ones you can rely on is at www.ampsoft.net/webdesign-l/WindowsMacFonts. html. A few of these are decorative, one is Comic Sans (no!) and some are unusable system fonts, leaving a small number that are safe and either good or at least tolerable.

"Rule number one: don't use Comic Sans. No, really. Decorative fonts should be used very sparingly, if at all."

Choosing how to host your site

Web pages are made up of text, image and media files that are stored on a server and viewed through a browser. In effect, your site is a document that the user opens, and it needs to be stored somewhere anyone can access. There are three choices: shared servers, dedicated servers and virtual private servers.

With all types of hosting, you're paying a company to store your website on a server, on their premises, connected to the internet. You produce the necessary files using whatever web design software you prefer (or pay someone else to do this) and upload them to the server, where other users can access them by entering your web address into their browser. Factors that affect what you can and can't achieve with your site include the speed and reliability of the server and what types of content it supports.

The differences between the three basic types of hosting arrangement are as follows.

Shared
As the name suggests, this is where you share a server with dozens, hundreds or even thousands of other websites.

With shared hosting, your site is stored on the same computer as many others, in much the same way you might run several programs at once on your PC. This limits performance, but reduces the price.

Shared hosting is the cheapest option and, usually, the easiest to set up, because you're not taking control of a computer, just adding your files to one that's already set up. On the other hand, the fact that you're sharing the web server means your site's performance can be compromised by the sheer weight of traffic the server has to cope with. Even if only a few people are trying to view your pages, you're also affected by the number accessing the other sites that may be on the same server.

Having said that, a good-quality shared hosting plan is a perfectly sensible choice for many online businesses, including those selling products online or simply using the internet to publicise themselves. You don't have the level of control over your hosting that either VPSs or dedicated servers offer, but in many cases, you simply don't need it, and you might not have enough technical knowledge to take advantage of it if you did.

As you would expect, the quality of shared hosting varies hugely between providers and across their product ranges. A package costing £2.99 per month is likely to be aimed at "home" use. At that level, you could expect to be squashed on to a server with many hundreds of other sites and to have a very limited range of features. Most hosts also offer "business" packages, and these will include greater bandwidth allowances (so more people can access your site before you start incurring extra costs), more sophisticated management features and promises of better performance. Performance essentially is the difference between visitors seeing your website straight away or being left waiting while pages struggle to load.

Dedicated
A dedicated server is a physical machine leased in its entirety by you. You get complete control

over your machine through a browser-based control panel and root/admin-level access. These computers usually run either Linux or Windows Server.

Dedicated servers are much more expensive than shared hosting, with prices beginning at around £100 per month, but they're almost always the right choice if you're developing a web application. In other words, if your core product is delivered to the customer via the internet, rather than being a physical product that is merely ordered online, a dedicated server is likely to be the best choice. It's also worth considering for any kind of online store that aims to attract large numbers of customers, as a shared service is unlikely to cope with high demand, even in short bursts.

Virtual Virtual private servers (VPSs) sit between shared and dedicated hosting in their cost and features.

To you, they offer all the functionality of a dedicated server for a fraction of the price: indeed, what you get appears to be a dedicated server in every detail. In reality, a single computer is running several "virtual servers". Each copy of the server software thinks it's running on its own computer, but in fact the machine's processor is handling them all at

the same time, while each has its own hard disk partition. Since the physical resources of the server are shared between the virtual servers, you can expect to get less hard disk space, lower memory and some competition for processor time, reducing performance.

However, VPSs are an excellent halfway house between shared hosting and dedicated servers. For around £30 a month you get most of the benefits of dedicated hosting for a price closer to business class-shared hosting.

OPERATING SYSTEMS Now that you've decided which type of hosting to plump for, your next decision is which operating system your web server should run. In everyday computing, the vast majority of users choose Windows. The choice is far less clear-cut with web hosting. Linux has long been the dominant web server operating system; it's reliable, lightweight, free and, crucially, the native environment of many of the web's core technologies, including PHP and MySQL. You can get Windows versions of these, but my preference is to run them under their intended operating system. (Incidentally, while Apple's Mac OS X operating system – available only on Macs – accounts for a respectable minority of desktops, it's not very widely used for commercial web hosting; Mac ➜

The great thing about a good hosting service is that this chap, or someone like him, looks after the server that runs your website, so you don't have to.

→ fans are likely to pick Linux.) For myself, I always begin with the assumption that my web server will run Linux, and will only consider Windows if there is a compelling reason to do so. For example, if a web application needs Microsoft's .NET Framework to run, Windows is the only choice.

Bear in mind that your familiarity with desktop Windows is of precious little use when it comes to configuring a Windows-based web server. With both Windows and Linux, you're shielded from the complexities of the operating system by browser-based control panels, which allow you to handle most tasks through a clear, icon-based interface. I don't pretend to be a Linux expert, and I could count the number of times I've needed to resort to the command-line interface on the fingers of one hand in the four years we've had a dedicated server.

All things considered, if you intend to create a website to sell products or publicise your business, a Linux-based hosting product is almost always going to be appropriate – and indeed the vast majority of shared hosting plans feature Linux. If you're creating a web application, on the other hand, your choice will depend on the technology you plan to use: .NET applications require a Windows server, while most other commonly used technologies are more at home on a Linux box.

SPACE AND BANDWIDTH Hosting packages will include a predefined amount of hard disk space. Generally speaking, as you might guess, the more expensive the package, the more space you'll get. However, the majority of websites require very little space, so don't imagine that you need to pay for the kind of hard disk space on your web server that you might have in your desktop PC. Most sites will easily fit into a few hundred megabytes – even a media-heavy site such as PassYourTheory.co.uk needs less than 3GB in total – so disk space is not likely to be a deciding factor in choosing a host. Treat "unlimited space" offers, therefore, with the disdain they deserve: it's not something you need to pay extra for.

Hosting packages usually specify a maximum bandwidth. This is the total amount of traffic that your site is allowed to handle before excess charges apply. If you have a web page that contains 80KB of data, for example, then each time one person views that page they're using 80KB of your bandwidth allowance. As with hard disk size, you may be surprised by how little you need. You would need hundreds of gigabytes of bandwidth only if you were running a media-streaming service. As a very rough rule of thumb, you should typically be allowed ten times your hard disk space in bandwidth per month. Again, in practice the bandwidth allowance is likely to be so high that it's irrelevant when it comes to selecting a host.

TECHNOLOGY As a bare minimum, your shared hosting package should include PHP 5 (the programming language that adds dynamic functionality to web pages) and MySQL 5 (the most commonly used database), with permission to create one database. You might not know yet that you're going to need these technologies, but they cost nothing,

"Most websites require very little space – don't imagine you need the kind of hard disk space on your web server that you have in your PC."

Check ratings such as PC Pro's to pick a good web host, for example Memset or Zen, and choose a mid-range to top-end hosting option.

cPanel, installed on many servers, allows you to control the setup of your space and domain through an easy-to-use graphical interface.

offer the possibility to add functionality to your site without needing to change packages later and, crucially, are required if you want to install WordPress and many other web applications that can make creating your site easier.

You also need a control panel to configure your web space. The most popular one for shared hosting is cPanel, and I recommend also ensuring that Fantastico De Luxe is included in your package. This is a bolt-on that offers one-click installation of a number of web applications, including WordPress, various other content management systems, photo galleries and discussion boards. Find out more at www.netenberg.com/fantastico.php.

For dedicated servers, cPanel is joined by Plesk. You get far greater functionality than with a shared host, allowing you to make low-level changes to your system configuration. Just remember that with great power comes great responsibility…

SERVICE-LEVEL AGREEMENTS
For dedicated hosting or VPS, only consider providers who offer a guaranteed "service level". The most important component of this is the percentage of time over any particular month that you can expect your server to be working. While 99% might sound excellent, bear in mind that a 1% downtime is over seven hours per month. You should be looking for at least 99.9% guaranteed uptime for a dedicated or virtual private server.

With shared hosting, you're much less likely to find a quoted figure. I suggest contacting the host's helpdesk (which in itself will tell you something about their responsiveness) and ask if they have a guaranteed uptime, or failing that if they can tell you what their uptime has been in, say, the past year. You can't expect quite such a high level with shared hosting, since you're paying so much less.

CONTRACT LENGTH There's no reason to sign up for more than a month-by-month commitment if you're intending to use shared hosting or a VPS. Avoid any host that doesn't at least offer the option of a monthly contract. With dedicated servers, it's more common to have an initial commitment of 12 months followed by an agreement to give one month's notice to terminate. Be very wary of signing up for longer to get a bigger discount – you don't know if this host is going to suit you yet.

EMAIL HANDLING Make sure, before you select a shared hosting package, that it includes enough email addresses. To have any credibility, you need to be able to send and receive emails from an address that includes your domain name. The days of being able to get away with an AOL or Hotmail email address are now long gone.

Case study
4: Buying a hosting package

With MakingYourOwnCandles.co.uk, we ruled out a dedicated server (at least initially) on cost grounds. At this early point, despite all our research, we can't guarantee that the income from the site and the traffic that comes with it will make a dedicated server worthwhile in the reasonably foreseeable future.

This does mean storing up a potential problem for later: if the site is a massive success, we might need to move across to a dedicated server, and this is not an easy process.

That left us with a choice between a VPS and shared hosting. Memset's "Miniserver" VPS started at around £16.50 (£19 inc VAT) per month including cPanel, while Zen's nearest equivalent shared hosting plan was £12 (£14 inc VAT). We finally decided on the cheaper option, because we don't anticipate needing administrator access to our server and because we're not going to be hosting our shop on the site. Had our product been a web application, we would certainly have gone for a dedicated server, which I think offers the ideal compromise between performance, features, control and cost.

MAKING THE DECISION The single best way to choose a host is through experience – either your own or that of people you respect. The PC Pro Awards (www.pcpro.co.uk/html/awards-2009) bring together the experience of thousands of readers, so that's a good place to start.

For the past four years, Memset (www.memset.com) has won the PC Pro Web Host award, and in the past three years Zen Internet (www.zen.co.uk) has twice achieved a Highly Commended runners-up spot. In the most recent year of the awards, Fast2host (www.fast2host.co.uk) won Highly Commended.

Based on these results, if you're looking for shared hosting your first port of call should be Zen (since Memset and Fast2host don't offer shared hosting plans), with honourable mentions going to 1and1.co.uk, Heart Internet and Namesco. Along with Zen Internet, I use www.daily.co.uk for my shared hosting and have found it to be pretty good, so you might want to add this company to your list of potential hosts.

Whoever you choose, I strongly recommend you make sure that cPanel is included. As we've explained above, this enables you to manage every aspect of your web space without needing to resort to Linux commands. It's also a sign of quality shared hosting by a provider who has actually thought about how the space will be used.

For dedicated servers, I suggest you begin by looking at Memset's options, which start at lower prices than Zen's. You can see for yourself which providers rank poorly on the PC Pro Awards page, and I would avoid taking any risks: your web presence is too important.

Choosing and registering a domain name

Selecting a domain name is one of the most important decisions you'll make in setting up your business. Your web address is a crucial part of your brand, and might appear on everything from T-shirts to press releases. Most crucially, it plays an important role in your internet marketing.

If you've been following from the beginning, you'll know that your domain name should include your most important keywords, if possible. This is because of the way Google matches the text of ads (sponsored keywords) and indexed websites against the search terms that users type in.

Even though Google indexes the entire content of millions of websites, and can find words buried deep in their pages, the domain name of a site – much like the title of a book – is still the clearest guide to relevance. If a user searches for 'candle making', and the domain includes those words, that's a strong indication that it's relevant to this user, so Google will tend to place it higher up.

Not only that, but on Google results pages the terms that the user typed in will be highlighted in bold wherever they appear. If that means at least part of your domain name ends up in bold, it will make your ad or listing entry more likely to be spotted by the searcher.

TOP-LEVEL DOMAIN The top-level domain (TLD) is the final part of the web address, such as ".co.uk", ".com", ".net" or ".org". If you're aiming primarily at the UK market, it makes sense to choose .co.uk. For an international

audience you might consider .com but it depends on your intended identity. In your market, do you believe that being perceived to be a UK company will result in more sales? If you don't know, buy both .com and .co.uk and split-test them. You may want to use both anyway, if they're available.

The .net TLD was originally intended for ISPs and other networking companies, but there's no formal regulation on this, so it's a viable alternative if the .com address you want is unavailable. Personally, I'd only use .net if my product was tech-related. Not-for-profit organisations tend to be the main users of .org, another popular TLD. Again, there's no policing of this, but I'd avoid it unless you are a charity or public sector organisation.

SECOND CHOICES What if the domain name you want has already been taken? There are plenty of other TLD extensions you could use, including .me.uk, .net.uk, .biz, .mobi and .eu. Each name exists separately within each TLD, so if someone else already has mywidgetcompany.com, you can still register mywidgetcompany.co.uk, and so on.

However, unless you have a compelling reason to use these alternative TLDs, they should be avoided. There's little point in spending money marketing the name 'Kevin's Candles' if users who go to kevinscandles.com (the most obvious domain) will find a completely different company – particularly since this domain is also likely to rank highly in the Google results when people search for 'Kevin's Candles'.

For a business targeting users of mobile devices, .mobi might be justified; if you're a pan-European company or you sell into Europe, .eu is a valid choice. The TLD .biz was invented to provide an alternative to .com, but I know which one I'd consider had higher credibility.

If the exact domain name you wanted has gone, try putting the keywords in a different order or turning nouns into verbs. Also check whether the existing domain name owners are actually using it for anything: they might be persuaded to sell for a reasonable price.

Try to buy as many combinations of your keywords as possible, as well as covering the main TLDs. Domain names are cheap, so don't scrimp and regret it later.

I used Daily.co.uk for my domain name registration, as I found it competitively priced, reliable and easy to use. Once registered, your domains can be transferred into the care of your preferred web host. Alternatively, ask whether your host can register domains and how much it charges for this. Always check whether there'll be a fee if you later want to transfer the domain to a different host.

1 **SEARCH THE WEB** Begin by searching for your chosen domain name at www.daily.co.uk or another registration service to see if it's available. At this point you should be looking for all reasonable combinations, so that if your research leads you to a different name later, there's a chance you've already bagged it. Notice here that one of the two domains I've already added to my shopping basket includes hyphens. This is because the unhyphenated version had already been taken. There's also an argument that it might actually be easier to read.

Making a mark

Whether a domain is available is not the only consideration. You should also ensure your business name doesn't infringe an existing trademark, or you could face legal action. You can check UK trademarks at www.ipo.gov.uk/tm/t-find/t-find-text, and US ones at http://tess2.uspto.gov. The catch is that these lists aren't comprehensive. Searching the web for all combinations and variations of your intended name is also sensible. If the .com or .co.uk address is already in use, think about whether that company might object if you start up in business at the .net or .biz equivalent. As a rule, a name that's unique in its market, such as Amazon, will be protected, while a descriptive name, such as Lots of Cheap Books, may not be.

2 **UK OR US?** There are many TLDs. I avoid all but the most common for commercial sites. I'm looking for .co.uk where it's a UK business selling to a regional audience (as with www.makingyourowncandles.co.uk), or .com for an international business. While most .com domains are registered by US companies, .com doesn't necessarily imply a US base.

3 **DEVIL IN THE DETAIL** Make certain you get the registration details correct. If the domain is to be owned by your limited company, that should be reflected here, but otherwise register it to yourself. Bear in mind that domain names can have a value, sometimes quite unexpectedly, so make sure you stand to get the benefit.

4 **GET YOUR WALLET OUT** Time to pay up! Fortunately, domain names are cheaper than they've ever been. Those ending in .co.uk cost only a few pounds per year, which makes it worth registering as many as possible. These domains are registered for two years, after which you can renew them. Others can be registered for longer, but I tend to stick to two years; after that, you might not want the domain any more.

How to set up your web space

So you've registered your domain name and chosen a host for your website. Here's how to get your web space ready.

I'm using shared hosting with Zen Internet (www.zen.co.uk). A shared hosting plan will generally have a default web address something like yourusername.webhost.co.uk. So, having registered your own domain, you need to arrange things so that typing this into a browser points to your web space.

1 **DNS** First go to your domain name registrar (in my case www.daily.co.uk) and change the DNS records for your domain to point to the IP address you've been given by your host. The "MX records" section handles email routing, so you should usually enter your default web address here. This done, click Update DNS. Bear in mind DNS changes can take many hours to take effect.

2 **POINT AND CLICK** Now go to cPanel in your shared hosting plan. Click Parked Domains, type your domain name and click Add Domain. Your domain name will now point to your shared hosting space.

To copy files to this space you'll need an FTP account. If you're only hosting one domain in your web space, you might as well use the default FTP account details that your host will have provided you with. If you don't

have any FTP software, head over to filezilla-project.org and download the free FileZilla FTP client, which we'll use now.

3 **CONNECT** Click File, Site Manager, New Site. Enter the default domain provided by your web host, then the FTP user name and password. Click Connect and your site should open in the file browser interface. Now open Notepad and type the following:

```
<h1>Any heading you like</h1>
<p>This proves that my site works</p>
```

and save it as index.html. Copy this to your website's root folder – usually /public_html or /httpdocs – via FTP.

4 **HEAD HOME** Now type your domain name into a web browser. You should see your simple home page. It may not look exciting, but it's proved your setup has worked. If you get a DNS error, try typing in your default web address instead. If the page appears here, either you've messed up your DNS settings or you need to wait a few minutes. If it doesn't appear, go to FileZilla and make sure you've copied the file into the right folder.

Creating a site using WordPress

WordPress is becoming an increasingly popular tool for creating a website quickly without needing specialist knowledge. And best of all, it costs nothing. Here we'll show you how to get it installed and working, and on the following pages we'll cover the basics of editing your site's look and feel.

Start by downloading the WordPress code, free of charge, from www.wordpress.org. (Don't confuse this with www.wordpress.com, where you can use the same technology to create a more limited site on WordPress's own server.) Download the Zip file version to a temporary folder on your PC, then extract the file into its own folder. If you don't have a Zip tool, the excellent 7-Zip can be downloaded free from www.7-zip.org.

1 CREATE YOUR DATABASE As we've mentioned, WordPress is a content management system (CMS). With a CMS, you store your content in a database from which it's retrieved, and displayed within a web page template, when visitors access your site. Your first step is to set up this database: specifically, a MySQL database on your web server.

To do this (assuming, again, that your web space includes the cPanel user interface; others may vary), go to www.yourdomainname.co.uk/cpanel – replacing "yourdomainname" with the domain you've now set up and pointed to your web space – and type in your cPanel username and password. Click the MySQL databases

icon and enter a name for your new database, such as "wordpress". Click Create Database. You also need to create a user account to access the database. Yet another login to remember? Yes, but you'll only ever need this to enter into WordPress when you first set it up; as long as you note the details somewhere in case of emergencies, you can then forget them. Enter a username, such as "wpuser", and a password, then click Create User. Bear in mind that cPanel may add your cPanel login name to the front of the username and database name. For example, if your login was jsmith, your username – assuming you'd typed "wpuser" – would be jsmith_wpuser.

2 ADD USERS Further down the same page, assign this user to your database. Select the user from the left-hand drop-down and the database from the right-hand list, and click Add User To Database.

We now need to enter these details into WordPress. Open up the folder on your computer containing the WordPress source files you downloaded. Find a file called "wp-config-sample.php" and rename it to wp-config.php. Open it in Notepad or another text editor (such as PSPad).

Find the following line:

```
define('DB_NAME', 'putyourdbnamehere');
```

Now replace "putyourdbnamehere" with the name of the database you just created, such as "wordpress". Note that you need the single quotation marks shown. On the following lines, replace "usernamehere" with your MySQL username (such as "wpuser") and "yourpasswordhere" with your MySQL password. Save the file.

In FileZilla, copy all the files in the /wordpress folder via FTP to the root of your website; or, if you want to set up a blog within a site, create a subfolder.

Run the installer by opening the file /wp-admin/install.php within your website root folder. (Note that if you haven't put the WordPress files in the root folder, you'll need to add the subfolder to this address, for example yourwebsiteaddress/blog/wp-admin/install.php.) On the install screen, give your blog a title, enter your email address and click the Install button. If you don't see this screen, pay attention to any error messages and fix them first.

Within a few moments you'll see the Success message. You'll be given the username "admin" and a randomly generated password. Make a note of it and copy it to the clipboard (highlight it and press <Ctrl-C>). Click Log In. Type "admin" in the Username box and the password in the other field (press <Ctrl-V> to do this). Click Log In again.

You should see a message at the top prompting you to change your password to something easier to remember. If not, this can be done on your Profile page.

3 **APPLY A THEME** On your WordPress Dashboard, click Visit Site at the top and you'll see a plain, boring, standard WordPress web page. Before we go any further, we'll find a theme to give our site a more appropriate and engaging look and feel. WordPress has thousands of free and paid-for themes available; if you can't find one that's perfect for your needs immediately, you can edit it or swap it for another later.

Click Site Admin to go back to the Dashboard. Click Appearance, Add New Themes. Use the "feature filter" to reduce the number of themes to choose from: tick some boxes and click Find Themes. For most purposes a two-column layout is ideal; you could also choose an appropriate colour. Having found a theme, click Preview to see how it looks, then Install. You'll be asked for your FTP information (the same as you used to connect in FileZilla). Click Proceed.

If this doesn't work – it might say it can't find wp-content, for example – you can do it manually. Go to http://wordpress.org/extend/themes and type the name of the theme you wanted. Click Download and save the Zip file. Unzip it and copy the entire folder (including its containing folder) via FTP into the wp-content/themes folder.

Either way, back at your Dashboard, click Appearance/Themes and you should see your new theme.

4 **THE END RESULT** Click Activate and then Visit Site and you should see your new website in all its glory. Unless you're astonishingly lucky, though, this site won't yet be absolutely right for you. You'll need to spend a little time tweaking its settings and appearance. Fortunately, as we'll see on the next page, this is surprisingly easy for non-experts to do.

So many WordPress themes are available that there's bound to be one suitable for your business. More can be found via Google, including sophisticated and professional paid-for themes that cost only a few dozen dollars.

3

4

Editing your WordPress site design

One of the joys of WordPress is that you can edit your theme to get the look you want. Your site is made up of PHP for the functionality and MySQL for the content, while CSS defines the appearance. Because these are all separate, you can change the look completely without any knowledge of MySQL or PHP.

Most WordPress themes are designed for blogs, so you may want to edit your theme to make it more like a shopping site. This will involve turning off features and services such as the RSS feed and comments. Each function is controlled by one CSS rule, so you can change the whole site just by deleting one line of code.

The Web Developer toolbar for Firefox provides all sorts of extra data about a web page, including detailed CSS information. You can find it at http://addons.mozilla.org.

In WordPress, go to the Dashboard and create your home page: remember it must be a page, not a post.

1 EDIT YOUR WIDGETS Widgets are plugins available with the standard WordPress installation. They typically appear in sidebars on your site and allow you, for example, to list pages and posts.

For a website, you're likely to need a list of pages plus the "Meta" widget, which allows you to log in and edit the site.

Under Appearance in your WordPress Dashboard, you can see a list of Widgets on the left and where they can appear on the right. In this example there are four possible locations, but this will depend on your theme. To add a Widget, drag and drop it from the left-hand panel to one of the locations on the right. To remove it, reverse the process.

Because of the way WordPress themes work, you may find some Widgets appear by default although they're not listed here. If you want to remove all Widgets from a location, the only way may be to add a blank Widget to override the default. The best choice is the Text Widget. Drag and drop this into any locations you want to be blank; as long as you don't enter any text into the Widget, nothing will be visible. It's a bit cack-handed, but it works.

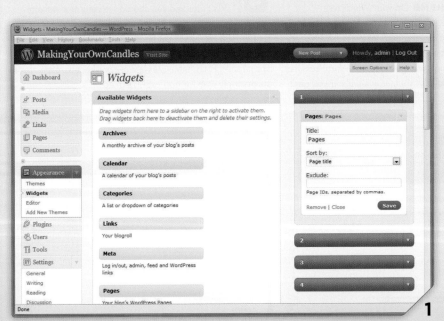

Widgets provide an easy way to add functionality to your website, but for a straightforward sales site you may not need them. Fortunately, like most other things in WordPress, they're simple to manage.

1

2

NO COMMENT
Use the "Find in page" function in Firefox to find the CSS rule name; I searched for ".nocomments". We're looking for a rule that applies only to .nocomments. If it's a combined rule, with other elements alongside it, we won't modify it because that would change all those elements. Modify the line to match the following text, or if there's no rule just for .nocomments, create one by adding the text:

2 EDIT THE CSS WordPress makes it possible to edit the CSS for your site through the Dashboard. If you're going to be making major changes you might prefer to use an editor such as PSPad, but the built-in editor is sufficient for most purposes.

Take a look at your site as it stands by clicking Visit Site. I suggest opening it in a separate window or tab for convenience; you can do this by clicking the link with the right mouse button and choosing the relevant option.

By default, WordPress allows visitors to add comments on any page or blog entry. This isn't appropriate to a sales website, so go to Settings > Discussion and make sure "Allow people to post comments on new articles" is deselected. Now, though, "Comments are closed" will appear on your page, so you'll need to delve into CSS to remove it.

On the Web Developer toolbar in Firefox, click the CSS button and choose View Style Information. An info bar appears under the toolbar, and when you move your mouse pointer over the web page, the Web Developer toolbar shows the CSS style name of the area under your pointer. Clicking brings up the specific CSS rules that apply to it.

In the screenshot (above right), we've highlighted the location of the mouse pointer and the CSS rule name: p .nocomments. To make the "Comments are closed" message invisible, we just need to change the rule. Go to Appearance > Editor in the Dashboard; the main stylesheet (style.css) will be loaded by default, and is usually the file you want. You may see a message at the bottom of this page telling you to make the file writable if you want to edit it. If so, run FileZilla, go to the /wp-content folder of your site, find the /theme subfolder and, within it, right-click the style.css file. Select File Permissions, and in the Numeric Value field type "666" (I kid you not!) and click OK. Then reload the editor page in WordPress – just click Firefox's Refresh button – and you should find an Update File button has appeared.

`.nocomments { display:none; }`

4 HEY PRESTO Click Update File. Reload your home page and you should find the comment message has disappeared. In my experience, this technique of hiding unwanted elements using CSS is the one you'll use most often. You can edit the main CSS file in the same way to make other changes to the style rules.

3

4

Getting it written

Ask any freelance web designer and they'll tell you that, while their clients are happy to lavish plenty of time and effort on the look and feel of their shiny new site, they'll pay almost no attention to getting the words right. This is partly because design is sexier; partly because the bulk of the design work is done by the designer, while the writing needs input from the business owner; and partly because writing is hard.

I can't tell you how important it is to get the words right, particularly on your home page and sales landing pages. No matter how impressive the design of your website or how effective it is from a usability point of view, poorly chosen or badly written copy is the fastest way to encourage your potential customer to click the Back button rather than take the action you want.

To make sure your words are working for you, here are my top seven tips for successful copywriting.

1 It's your job

While it's fine to hire an external copywriter, the responsibility for getting the copy *right* is yours alone. One test of a good copywriter is that they will ask to spend a lot of time with you to understand your business and

customers before they write a single line. Either way, the process will involve a lot of your time and effort: this isn't something you can abdicate responsibility for.

Why? First, because it's your business and – just as you'll be heavily involved in selecting or building the product or service you sell, and you'll be making dozens of key decisions as you develop your business – your intimate knowledge is essential to defining the message you're presenting to your potential customers.

And second, because the quality of your copy could make the difference between profit and loss, between success and failure. This means that when you're deciding on your priorities, copywriting should be right at the top. Because it's so critical, you can't expect someone else to bring the same level of commitment and knowledge to the

process as you can yourself. That's not to say you can't or shouldn't hire a copywriter to help polish the wording, but the bulk of the work needs to be done by you.

2 Know your customer

Probably the biggest mistake you'll see in web copy is that writers have written it for themselves rather than for their target audience. Clearly, your audience isn't you: after all, you don't need to buy your product.

If you've been following the advice so far, you will have carried out a survey to help with your product development. The results of this survey will help you understand the characteristics of your audience. Not only

> **"We aimed our driving test site at 17-19s. It turns out that this group are already confident of passing and expect to get everything free."**

will you learn what they're looking for in their purchase but, if you included any open-ended questions, you'll also be familiar with the sort of language they use – and, indeed, how many of them don't have English as a first language, which will affect the way you write your copy.

My company launched the subscription-based driving theory test website PassYourTheory.co.uk in 2005. At the time, we didn't conduct a pre-launch survey, although we've run many surveys subsequently to learn how to improve the product. We thought we already knew who our target audience was.

After all, isn't it obvious? You might well assume, for example, that a driving theory test website should be aimed at 17- to 19-year-olds, so we designed the site – and wrote our copy – to appeal to this age range.

However, subsequent surveys have shown us that while we might get a lot of traffic from this age group, the people who actually buy from us tend to be older, and our most profitable customers are in their late twenties and disproportionately female.

Some of the things we discovered were that 17- to 19-year-olds expect to get everything for free and that they're supremely confident about passing their tests with a minimum of effort. So they don't see the need for tuition products and have no inclination to pay for them. In retrospect this may seem unsurprising, but our choice to aim our product at them seemed logical, if uninformed, at the time. As it happens, many competitors have come and gone over the years, and in each case they've been aimed at teenagers. We know what they were doing wrong.

Learning this about our target audience changed everything when it came to presentation and, critically, copy. Our surveys and other analysis have also discovered what specific needs our customers have when it comes to theory test training, and this now informs both our product offering and our copy.

If a potential customer has a need in mind when they type their search term into Google, and they see that need reflected in the Google Ad that comes up and then reflected again in the page they arrive at when they click it, they're much more likely to buy.

To demonstrate this, I conducted a test (you'll see how to do this in part 3 of this book) comparing the effectiveness of a specialised landing page with the standard "one size fits all" home page. Within a day, Google had produced enough data for me to be certain that I had a winner: the landing page outperformed the home page by more than 65%. And the only significant difference between the two was the copywriting.

The moral of the story is that you should learn as much about your customers as you can. Write directly for them. Anticipate what's likely to be on their mind when they reach your site, and reflect that. Relevance is everything. ➜

Copywriting is one of the hardest and most critical jobs in putting together your web presence. Even if you hire a professional to polish your words, it's up to you to figure out how best to address your visitors and turn as many as possible into buyers.

3 What's in it for them?

When visitors to your site read your copy and evaluate your offer, the question they'll be asking themselves is: "What's in it for me?" While a website is designed to be visited by many thousands of people, for each visitor the experience is a personal one. Just as with a book, the conversation is essentially one-to-one: you are talking directly to the reader.

Having learned something about your target audience, you need to write your copy so that this audience sees the benefits in your products compared to those of your competitors. You must present your products in terms of *benefits*, as opposed to its features and their advantages.

Here's an example. Let's imagine you go to a PC superstore to buy a new laptop. The clichéd portrayal (also sadly realistic) of the computer salesperson is that they'll bombard you with facts – usually read direct from the point-of-sale labels – without any explanation.

"It has a 160 gigabyte hard disk" is a feature. "Which means there's enough space to store around 80,000 photos or 30,000 music tracks" is an advantage. But what's the benefit? Perhaps: "So it has plenty of space for normal purposes and won't need to be upgraded in the near future." (OK, for the pedantic, that's two benefits).

All the user cares about is that the hard disk is big enough. By putting the feature in context with the advantage, and explaining what the consequence of the feature is (with the benefit), not only is the user's concern allayed but the reason to buy the product is comprehensibly and plausibly explained.

A useful way to present your Feature-Advantage-Benefit information is to use the linking words: "Has

[feature]. Which [advantage]. So [benefit]." Remembering the "so" is critical, as it ensures you are explaining what the benefit means, not assuming your customers can work it out for themselves.

Some more examples:

PassYourTheory.co.uk **has** a unique hazard perception walkthrough **which** guides you through a typical clip pointing out when to click, **so** you can approach your test with complete understanding and confidence.

This book **has** a section on copywriting **which** explains the key principles of good copy **so** you can avoid typical beginner's mistakes and save money.

4 What do you want them to do?

You should know what you want your customer to do, whether that's buy a product immediately, ask for more information or sign up for a mailing list. But does your customer know? Never assume that this is obvious: make it crystal clear what action you expect them to take, as many times as possible.

It's essential that you have this action "above the fold". This means it will appear on your web page without the viewer needing to scroll down, because some may not get as far as scrolling. The problem, of course, is that there's a huge range of resolutions on PC screens. Gone are the days when almost everyone was using 1,024x768; most new monitors are widescreen, some are as big as 30 inches, and at the other end of the scale there are mobile devices and netbooks with various formats and resolutions.

For most purposes, your "buy" button or signup area can be placed at around 500 pixels down the page and you'll know that the vast majority of your audience will see it without scrolling. However, if you're targeting mobile users you would need to think about placing the button higher and testing the site on multiple devices.

5 Keep it simple

There's no avoiding the importance of simple, clear, grammatically correct English. Irritating though it may be to many entrepreneurs, getting this right will have a direct impact on your conversion rate (how many visitors go on to buy something). Remember you are communicating more than just a message in your copy; your words also represent your product. If your copy contains grammatical

65% more people responded to this landing page than to our home page. Note the call to action "above the fold" (in blue).

Term	Found in (HTML elements)						Importance (Relative to other terms)
1. test	p (20x)	strong (6x)	h1 (2x)	title tag (1x)	li (1x)	h2 (1x)	100%
2. hazard	p (8x)	strong (4x)	li (2x)	title tag (1x)	h2 (1x)	h1 (1x)	95%
3. perception	p (7x)	strong (4x)	li (2x)	title tag (1x)	h2 (1x)	h1 (1x)	95%
4. theory	p (13x)	title tag (2x)	h1 (2x)	strong (2x)			77%
5. training	p (4x)	strong (2x)	li (2x)	title tag (1x)			58%

"In the past, marketers crammed their web pages with search terms, often invisibly. If you try this now you will end up blacklisted."

errors and spelling mistakes, that suggests to many buyers that you're careless, so they're unlikely to buy from you.

Follow a ruthless and rigorous editing process. Begin by getting all your thoughts written down. Apply all the tips given here through a series of drafts until you get to your final version. This version will almost always end up much shorter than the first. Every paragraph, every sentence, every word must serve the purpose of making it more likely that your audience will buy your product or service. Any words that aren't relevant are not only wasted, they make it more likely that you'll lose the reader's attention before they decide to buy something.

Re-read your copy, asking yourself whether your visitors really need to know everything you've included.

6 Be friends with Google

Google rewards relevance. Why? Because it's what searchers want. The more relevant Google believes your web pages to be, the better they will rank and the cheaper your advertising will be.

Google determines relevance primarily from the websites that link to you (and those that you link to) and from the content on the page. At the most elementary level, it will compare the copy on the page with the search phrase

that the user typed in. In the dim and distant past of the early 2000s, this led to internet marketers cramming their pages with search terms, often invisibly. Google is far too sophisticated to tolerate this sort of behaviour now, and if you try these dated techniques you will end up blacklisted.

The secret to a good ranking is to write copy that your target audience will appreciate. That's pretty much it: no black hat techniques are required. A well-structured site will result in landing pages that are naturally closely matched to the keywords visitors have typed in. Google will see these pages as relevant and reward you accordingly.

7 Get your headline right

The most important line of your copy is the first one visitors see. Headlines fall into several types, including questions ("How much is peace of mind worth to you?"), calls to action ("Sign up now for free peace of mind") and direct headlines ("Free peace of mind here"). One of the most popular is the "how to" ("How to get free peace of mind in seconds").

The best headlines grab the user's attention with something either interesting or too good to pass over. If you need some inspiration, have a look through Jay Abraham's "100 Greatest Headlines Ever Written" at www.pcpro.co.uk/links/headlines.

Images and graphics

No web page is complete without at least one image. Can you remember the last site you visited that had none? But they need to be used with care, and you need to be clear why you're using them. To help you choose wisely, bear in mind that images fall into three types: branding, illustrative and decorative.

Branding Your logo is an essential part of your brand, and you need it to work well and look professional.

Trying to get a logo developed on the cheap is a false economy. MakingYourOwnCandles.co.uk needed a logo, and I made the mistake of using an online logo company that charges only £25. The results were absolutely diabolical. After eight rounds of amendments it was still diabolical. The only aspect I liked was the typeface, which turned out to be available as a free font, so I paid the money, took the design, deleted everything but the text and added the graphical element myself.

On a later project, I used 99designs.com. With this service, and others like it, you set up a competition and designers from around the world compete to come up with a winning design. There's a minimum prize fund of around £175, which, believe me, is very reasonable. So reasonable, in fact, that it may not attract experienced professional designers, but you do have the benefit of opening up your job to people from countries with lower wage expectations. I had a very successful experience on this occasion and was delighted with the results. It's also possible to set up contests for the design of entire websites, but I don't recommend this, because web design involves a lot more interaction between you and the designer than a logo does.

If you're prepared to invest a little more money in your "corporate identity", there are plenty of UK-based graphic designers who can oblige. Ask around locally for recommendations or search the web; the best approach is to find existing work that you like, then find out who designed it (if the graphics aren't credited, the site owner may not mind telling you who did them) and ask them to quote for what you need. Professional designers will expect a clear brief and will not usually be prepared to work "on spec"; if you commission work from professionals, you will have to

> "Trying to get a logo developed on the cheap is a false economy. I paid only £25 and the results were diabolical."

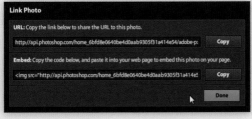

Photoshop.com offers a sophisticated image editor free of charge. It works entirely online, via your web browser, and is especially suitable for editing photos for websites because you won't need to work with high-resolution files that take ages to upload and download.

You can use free space on sites such as Photoshop.com to store photos and insert them into your web pages using links (above) without having to host them on your own web server.

pay for it, though you can ask for changes, within reason. Be wary of agencies, as opposed to invidual designers. They can help guide you through the process, but will cost a lot more and may pressurise you to spend more than you need to.

Other graphics on your site should also reflect your branding, at least in their colours and ideally in style.

Illustrative

Illustrative graphics are photographs and other images depicting the product itself.

They might be photos of a physical product or screenshots of software. For a service, you might include photos of customers alongside their testimonials. If your product needs explaining or demonstrating, you might need to get diagrams drawn.

When taking photos of your product, I recommend investing in proper lighting and a light cube. These can be bought at low cost from eBay and, along with a tripod and a reasonable camera (I use a Sony Alpha a200 entry-level DSLR, but a digital compact will do fine) you can achieve impressive results. Good-quality product shots increase your customers' perception of your professionalism, which means you will make more sales for higher prices.

For screenshots, you can't beat the low-cost Snagit from Techsmith (www.techsmith.com/snagit) which also includes an editor that offers batch image processing.

Decorative

Any graphic that doesn't either enhance your brand or illustrate your product or service needs to be treated with caution.

Images with no purpose serve only to distract visitors from the parts of the page you want them to concentrate on. If it doesn't have a reason to be there, get rid of it.

SOURCING IMAGES If you need photos of your specific product, you'll have to get them from your supplier or take them yourself. Generic photos and graphics can come from other sources. Don't steal them from other people's websites: quality may be compromised and you could get sued for copyright infringement. (This really does happen, and the costs are far higher than buying the images in the first place.) There are plenty of free or low-cost "stock" and clip-art libraries. A good source is www.clipart.com, which includes illustrations, photos and photo objects (pictures of things on a transparent background). Of the stock

Moving images

I'm struggling to think of an animation that actually enhanced the website it was on. Some sites are created entirely in Flash, but as well as requiring more design skills this makes it harder to achieve high search-engine rankings. Dropping animation into an HTML page is rarely a good idea, because most web users now equate animation with adverts and will ignore it. Don't use animation just to show off, and *never* as a lead-in to your site. The dreaded "skip intro" link was never a good idea.

If you have a good reason for including animation, the only format to use is Flash SWF. You don't need to buy Adobe's Flash application to create animations; the best tools I've seen are SWiSH Max and miniMax (www. swishzone.com), as used for the spinning globe above, which offer much of the functionality of the Flash authoring tool at a lower cost.

image libraries, my favourite is www.fotolia.com; an image suitable for web use costs either 75p or £1.50 depending on its size, so it's hardly going to break the bank. Another popular choice is www.istockphoto.com. You can buy images individually or by subscription; the latter is intended for people who regularly need more content, but you could spend time selecting a set of images and then sign up for a short period and download them all.

My favourite photo editor is Adobe Photoshop Elements. If you're going to be creating your own videos, it makes sense to buy it in a bundle with Premiere Elements. Having said that, if you're only likely to edit a limited number of images, you might be able to make do with the online version of Photoshop Elements (www.photoshop. com), which is free. This allows you to perform basic edits and then either link to the image on Adobe's servers or download it for uploading via WordPress. Alternatively, there's Google Picasa (http://picasa.google.co.uk), a free editing program with a growing number of useful functions.

You should always save images at the exact size you want them to appear on your site, in pixels, rather than relying on setting their width and height properties in HTML. This ensures the image files are no larger than necessary and quality isn't lost when browsers downsize them. Most images should be saved in JPEG format, and you'll need to adjust the compression settings so that the image still looks good but is as small in file size as possible.

FILE FORMATS There are three file formats widely used on websites – JPEG, PNG and GIF – and it's usually pretty easy to work out which would be the best for your purposes. For an icon or diagram with relatively few colours, or a simple design with no gradient fills, consider GIF. These files support only 256 colours (including one transparent colour) and compress to small sizes. GIF is a good choice if your image is black and white, even if it's a photo.

If you have a full-colour picture that needs to support transparency, PNG is your only choice. For example, although most photos include backgrounds and are inserted into the site as a rectangle, some – described as "photo objects" or "isolated" – are designed to have a transparent background. This may be supplied as a "clipping path" or "alpha channel", but you'll need to load the image into a photo editor and save it as a PNG to make the transparency work when the image is included in a web page.

In just about every other case, JPEG is the right format. It tends to offer better compression than PNG while supporting more colours than GIF. However, JPEG doesn't support transparency. It's completely supported in all browsers, whereas older versions didn't handle PNGs well. So your default choice should be JPEG, with the others only being selected for specific purposes.

Video and sound

Used appropriately, sound and video can enhance your site's message. Used poorly, they can drive away visitors in an instant. Here we'll find out what are the top irritations and what really works, and see how to add audio and video to a WordPress site.

The most important thing to remember when adding "rich media" to your site is to make sure playback is under the control of your visitor. There are few things more annoying, or more likely to lead to the visitor clicking the Back button, than a sound file or video that auto-plays as soon as the user arrives at your page.

Having said that, well-produced video and audio can be excellent attention-grabbers for your most important messages. As a rule, video or audio is used on a landing page to reinforce the main purpose of that page, which is usually to get a visitor's email address or initiate a sale. Rich media is likely to be less welcome on your home page or other information-rich pages within your site, since when a visitor is viewing those pages they're likely to be looking for something specific, and it's much quicker to do so in text and graphics, which are all visible immediately, than in a video, where you have to wait and see what appears.

SOUND: THE VOICEOVER Please don't use sound as a musical backdrop to your site: this breaks our first rule. Even if the site is promoting a band, samples of your music should be controllable by the visitor – and by that I do *not* mean you start the music automatically and offer a Stop button. While this might be mildly acceptable the first time someone arrives at your site, can you imagine how irritating it will be a dozen visits later? Assuming they ever come back, which of course they won't.

A better use of sound is for speech. No matter how short your message, always write a script. This is the only way to make sure you say everything that needs saying without the otherwise inevitable "ums" and "ahs".

Sound can be deployed as a widget built into your site, with a playback bar giving the visitor control. More often than not, this widget will be Flash or JavaScript-based and the sound will be in MP3 format.

Recording speech requires minimal equipment and software. I strongly recommend investing in a decent microphone. Samson produces a range of USB microphones, available from audio stores such as www.dolphinmusic.co.uk from around £60, that dispense with the need for a mixing deck or pre-amp and plug straight into your PC. Avoid services that let you phone in your audio and receive it as an MP3 file: this is convenient for business tasks, but the quality is too low for recordings that you want to present to an audience.

The best choice among free audio-editing software is Audacity (http://audacity.sourceforge.net). Despite an interface out of the 1990s, it does a good job, and recording spoken audio isn't, after all, rocket science.

Having output your audio to MP3, you then need a way of embedding it in your page. For a self-coded site, my tool of choice is SWiSH Jukebox (www.swishzone.com), which takes an MP3 – or a series of MP3s – and outputs a Flash SWF file incorporating a customisable control bar.

Software and product demonstrations are an ideal use for video, whether on your own site or YouTube.

Here's the editor of *Wired* magazine popping up as a talking head to get his message across.

For a WordPress site, a number of plugins exist to host MP3s; my favourite, for its sheer simplicity, is WPaudio (http://wpaudio.com).

VIDEO: THE TALKING HEAD Generally speaking, video on sales websites takes two forms. First, there's the "talking head" beloved of internet marketing gurus. Typically this involves the site-owner talking directly into the camera, seeking to persuade visitors to sign up or buy a product. This can be effective since, done well, it can inject enthusiasm and dynamism into what otherwise might have been dry copy. It works especially well where there's no physical product that you can show off.

Second, and more rarely, you'll come across a video that shows a product being used. I expect this to become more common, especially on high-price items. Imagine, for example, how much more likely you'd be to buy an item you'd just seen opened and used in a video than one that's shown only as a box shot.

> "Video on your website can take one of two forms: the talking head and the product demonstration or presentation."

To make your video look professional, you need to pay attention to two things above all else: sound and light. Unless you're going for an "urban guerrilla" look, set up your camcorder on a tripod in a well-lit location. Natural sunlight is often best, and certainly cheapest, but otherwise you can get good results from a bright halogen uplighter, which creates a good lighting level without obvious shadows.

Recording sound on video can be tricky. If your camcorder has a mic input socket, a lapel microphone will work fine. If not, I recommend recording the sound separately using a digital dictaphone. Place it just out of view (or tape it to a broom handle and get someone to dangle it out of view, like in the movies) and you can then combine it with the video in an editing program such as Premiere Elements. It's a bit of extra work to get it synced, but the quality will be far better than with the internal mic.

Solid-state pocket camcorders such as the Flip Mino and Ultra (www.theflip.com) are increasingly popular. A standard-definition model – SD rather than HD – is fine, given that you'll only be able to use low-bandwidth video on your site. The only downside with these devices is that if you're filming yourself, there's no flip-out LCD panel to watch yourself while you record. A budget full-size digital camcorder is another option, with today's tapeless models making it almost as easy to import your footage.

DEMOS AND PRESOS
Computer-generated or presentational video is known in some quarters as "poor man's video", but can be extremely effective. For example, if you're selling a software product, you might create a screen-capture video showing the product in use, with accompanying narration.

While this is simpler to set up than a live "talking head" video, getting it right takes preparation and a script, since you don't want to record any mistakes. Camtasia Studio (www.techsmith.com/camtasia.asp) is my favourite tool for the job, as it's very simple to use and produces high-quality results. It's available on a fully functional 30-day trial.

You can also use Camtasia to capture a PowerPoint slideshow, add a voiceover and output the result as a video. This can work well, but remember that most presentations are boring even when given live, let alone on the web. I'm a firm believer in Guy Kawasaki's 10/20/30 rule: 10 slides in 20 minutes with no text at less than 30-point size (http://blog.guykawasaki.com/2005/12/the_102030_rule.html).

Don't use PowerPoint's built-in clip art – buy low-cost stock images, as described on pp74-75 – and try to avoid the built-in templates. Take the time to create your own and your video won't look like just another PowerPoint.

HOSTING VIDEO Once it's created, you'll need to decide whether you're going to host your own video content. If it's purely for use on your website, it makes sense to store it in your web space. However, if you've created a marketing video that would make sense independently of the site, hosting it elsewhere might be a way to drive traffic to your pages.

For example, a product or software demonstration video should be hosted on YouTube, so that people searching the site will find it. Having uploaded it to YouTube, you can also embed it in your site using the link that YouTube provides. Don't embed your own controller in the video, as YouTube adds its own. Just upload the movie to YouTube, and once it's live you can copy and paste the "Embed" code from its YouTube page into your HTML. ➜

Pocket camcorders such as the Flip offer a cheap and simple way to capture video for your website. Just make sure you pay as much attention to lighting and audio quality as you would when shooting in a professional format.

STEP BY STEP Adding audio content to a WordPress website

Audio content can help give your site the edge. Here's how to record, process and host your own audio.

Begin by downloading the free sound editor Audacity from http://audacity.sourceforge.net. Get the latest version and also, from the Optional Downloads section, the LAME MP3 encoder. Install Audacity and, once that's done, run the LAME setup program. This adds the MP3 export function to the software.

1 **RECORD** Run Audacity, connect a microphone to your PC and speak into it. You should see the level bar under the play/record controls fluctuate. If you're not seeing anything, you may need to change the default recording device in File > Preferences > Devices.

When you're ready, with your script in view, click the Record button and speak into the microphone clearly and slowly, but with some animation in your voice, not as if you're reading a will. Click the Stop button when you've finished. You can then trim the clip to the right length by dragging a selection box across the "lead in" and "lead out" points and pressing the Delete key on the keyboard.

Audacity also has tools for enhancing your recording. If you've used a cheap microphone or are in a noisy environment, try the noise reduction filter. To ensure that the volume will be reasonable on playback, click Effect > Normalize and enter a value of 1dB.

Once you've finished editing, go to File > Export, select MP3 as the format and click OK. Remember that the name you choose for the file will appear as part of the playback controller on your site, so make it appropriate.

Now log in to your WordPress Dashboard, go to Plugins > Add New and type "wpaudio" into the search box. This should present the WPAudio MP3 player as the only result. Click Install.

2 **UPLOAD AUDIO** Now create the page or post where you want the audio to appear. Click the media upload icon above the rich text editor. Browse for your file and upload it. Copy the "Link URL" into Notepad, ready to insert in your page later. Don't click "Insert into Post", as this would result in WordPress presenting the MP3 as a link. Instead, click Save all changes.

3 **CALL THE MP3 WIDGET** Back in Edit Post (or Edit Page), type the following code:

```
[wp audio url="http://yourmp3url"]
```

replacing "yourmp3url" with your Link URL. You can repeat the process to add as many MP3s as you like, along with any other content for the post or page.

4 **PLAY** Click Update Page (or Update Post) and Preview to see your MP3 widget. Once the user clicks the Play button, a clickable progress bar and duration information appears as your recording plays back.

1

2

4

Adding plugins to your WordPress site

WordPress allows you to add functionality to your site with a huge range of plugins. There are currently over 7,000 available, covering everything from polls to searchengine optimisation and even simple online shops. Most are free, although some have paid-for "premium" versions, and they can usually be installed at the click of a button.

Exactly which plugins you'll need will depend on the type of business you're setting up. If you're selling a physical product range, you might decide the plugins supplied with WordPress provide everything you need to get started. If you're setting up an information business, you might need a plugin that allows you to sell memberships that give access to restricted parts of the site. Even if you're only using your website to support either an offline business or an eBay business, you'll almost certainly find plugins that will make your site more effective.

PLUGINS EVERY SITE SHOULD HAVE All the following plugins can be downloaded via Plugins >Add New in your WordPress Dashboard. Enter a search term and select the plugin you want, then click Install. This will bring up a dialog box giving more information on the plugin.

Most plugins can be installed automatically by WordPress, but if not, in most cases all you have to do is download a Zip file, unzip it, then upload it via FTP, complete with its containing folder, to your /wp-content/plugins folder.

Once this is done, you'll find the plugin listed under Plugins > Installed. Click Activate and it will begin working. In most cases you'll need to configure it, and this is done under Settings in the Dashboard.

All in One SEO

We'll be covering search engine optimisation in the final part of this book. For now, suffice to say that when it comes to getting your site ranked highly by Google, and therefore noticed by customers, SEO is essential. As the leading plugin for this purpose, All in One SEO should be installed on any site you create in WordPress. It gives you the same control over SEO as you'd have if you created your own site from scratch.

Install the plugin, enable it and set the Home Title, Home Description and Home Keywords. As in our example (left), as a first pass you should simply ensure that your main keywords are included in all three fields while using natural language.

You've probably seen websites with text at either the beginning or end of the page containing the same keywords repeated endlessly. This is a very old-fashioned technique aimed at fooling search engine "spiders" into believing that the site is very relevant because the main keywords represent a high percentage of the total words on the page. However, Google and the other search engines have long since got wise to this, and now penalise such ham-fisted attempts to fool them.

The All in One SEO plugin makes it easy for you to ensure that your website is search-engine friendly.

Register Plus allows you to create customised user registration schemes, adding whatever items of personal data you want to collect.

Akismet

If you enable comments on your site, you'll soon realise that blog comment spam is as big a nuisance as email spam. "Comments" full of advertising or nonsense will quickly swamp your pages. Fortunately, WordPress makes it simple to tackle them through the Akismet plugin. This is normally installed when you set up WordPress, so all you need to do is activate and configure it. You'll need a WordPress.com API key; if you have an account with WordPress.com (remember this is different from WordPress.org, which you're using),

you'll find it in your Profile: if you don't, just follow the link to set one up – it's free. Once you have your API key, go to Plugins/Akismet Configuration, enter it and click Update. Akismet will then work on your behalf, eliminating the vast majority of spam comments so you don't have to.

Register Plus

In most cases you'll want visitors to register with your site. This is the simplest way to build a list of people interested in you and your products. In the next part of this book we'll look at setting up an email list, but the Register Plus plugin means you can immediately keep track of interested visitors from the moment you launch your site.

WordPress has a built-in registration function, but it's very basic. Register Plus allows you to add custom fields to the registration form so you can learn more about your visitors when they sign up. You can also let them set their own password up front (rather than having to use an auto-generated one and change it through their profile later), and you can replace the WordPress logo with your own.

Under Settings > Register Plus Settings you'll see a whole list of options. For now, make sure you tick "Allow New Registrations to set their own Password" and "Enable Password Strength Meter". If you have a logo, upload it here. Make sure you tick "Prevent fake email address registrations". The alternative is to enable Captcha image verification, where users have to type in words shown in a box, but I've found this confuses some people, and anything that puts off potential customers is to be avoided.

Use the User Defined Fields section to add any extra data you want to ask for. You might want to know the user's gender or age range, or what led them to your site. Don't ask superfluous questions; every question will reduce the number of people who bother to complete the process.

Exclude Pages

You'll also be creating pages that you don't want to be included in the standard site navigation. These will include "thank you" pages for purchasers and those that sign up to your mailing list along with landing pages. The "Exclude Pages from Navigation" plugin adds an "Exclude Pages" group to the "Edit Pages" screen. To make a page invisible to the navigation system, simply deselect "Include this page in user menus".

Custom Meta

The default Widget that contains the "log in/register" link isn't customisable and contains options that aren't appropriate to a standard website. Install the Custom Meta

---

Pick a plugin

When it comes to selecting a plugin, the key questions to ask (and all the answers should be in the plugin's page within the WordPress Plugin Directory) are:

- **Have lots of other people used it?**
- **Does it have a good rating?**
- **Is it being actively developed?**

You also need to check whether it's compatible with your installed version of WordPress. Be aware that WordPress issues updates to the core system very regularly, so I wouldn't worry if the plugin doesn't say it's compatible with the very latest version. For example, if you're using version 2.8.6, as long as the plugin states it's compatible up to, say, 2.8.4 then I wouldn't worry too much. You can, after all, uninstall a plugin at any time.

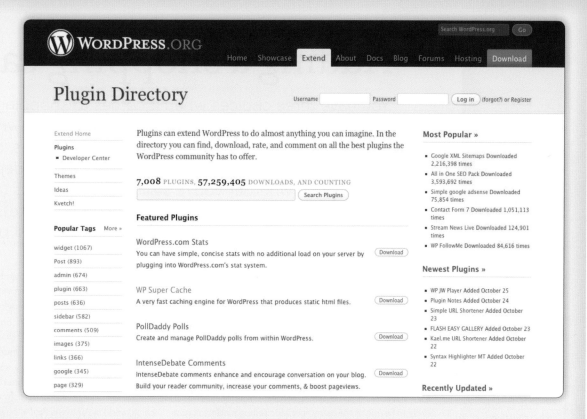

plugin and, unlike the others listed here, it will appear in your Dashboard under Appearence/Widgets. Find the Meta Widget and remove it, replacing it with the new Custom Meta widget. Give it a title such as "Log in" and select "Show 'Register/Site Admin'" and "Show 'Log in/Log out'" since these are the only relevant options.

OTHER USEFUL PLUGINS Given that there are over 7,000 plugins, you're likely to find something that meets your needs. The more specialised plugins tend to cost money, but it will be a fraction of the cost of creating an equivalent function from scratch.

MemberWing

As its name suggests, MemberWing is a membership manager. It allows you to protect parts of your site from non-members, and even put preview content in place which is then replaced with the real content when the user pays.

MemberWing is extremely sophisticated and includes integration with payment processors such as PayPal and Google Checkout, automatically adding new paid subscribers to the list of premium members and removing them when their payment expires. It also includes "drip feeding" of content, where pages are opened up over a period of time to each member. This is ideal for training sites where the course is delivered one week at a time.

If you don't need drip feeding, the Webmaster One version of the software ($99.99) is likely to fit the bill; otherwise, Professional One ($149.95) is the right choice.

WP Shopping Cart

This provides a shopping cart that integrates with your WordPress site and various payment gateways. It works well for a limited product range, but you may find it too limited if your business revolves around selling a range of products; on the following pages we'll look at more sophisticated shopping cart options.

WP Shopping Cart provides a straightforward way to take payment for products as long as your e-commerce requirements are fairly basic.

Adding a shopping cart

You have three choices when it comes to shopping carts: you can build your own from scratch, buy or download a pre-built system and adapt it to your purposes, or sign up for a third-party service. Your decisions will depend primarily on whether you're selling subscriptions (where members buy access to hidden parts of your site), software (which only buyers can download), or a physical product.

SUBSCRIPTIONS If you're selling subscriptions, you may need to build your own cart, since no two sites' requirements will be quite the same. Having said that, if you're simply protecting content from non-subscribers, then Amember (www.amember.com) is a good choice, and the WordPress plugin MemberWing (see p81) offers similar facilities as long as you can bend your site model to fit.

SOFTWARE If you're selling software, your best bet is likely to be one of the many specialist selling platforms such as www.regnow.com. These integrate payment with the emailing of registration details to buyers that enable them to unlock the product they've bought.

PHYSICAL If you're selling physical products, the choice is between hosting a payment system on your server or out-sourcing to a third party. osCommerce (www.oscommerce.com) is a PHP-based open-source ecommerce package that you download and install on your own server. It's a great choice if you have a wide range of products and are prepared to spend time configuring it so that it matches the look of your site and integrates with your payment processors.

If you want to get up and running quickly and you have a more limited product range – up to, say, 100 products – then a WordPress plugin should do the job. WP e-Commerce (also known as WP Shopping Cart) is a free plugin with additional modules that can be purchased later.

These solutions give your customers a way to select products. You then need a way of collecting their details and receiving money from them. The simplest choices are Google Checkout (http://checkout.google.co.uk) and PayPal (www.PayPal-business.co.uk). You'll need a Google Checkout Merchant account or a PayPal Business account respectively; both are easy to set up. In each case, a small sum of money is automatically deposited in your nominated bank account. This is used to verify that you own the account: to complete the setup, you're asked to type in the amount of the deposit that was made. You should allow two working weeks to complete the process.

Both Google Checkout and PayPal allow non-members to pay by credit card. However, PayPal traditionally doesn't allow a credit card that has been registered against a PayPal account to be used independently. So if you are a member, you can only pay via PayPal, not directly by card. This can cause confusion and irritation to customers, particularly if they've forgotten their PayPal details, so I suggest you add another provider besides Google Checkout and/or PayPal. For example, Nochex (www.nochex.co.uk) is a UK provider of secure payment processing. Although it offers customer accounts like PayPal, relatively few people have Nochex accounts, so you can simply use its credit card facility to offer users the option to pay directly by card, without much risk of their accounts clashing.

When we launched PassYourTheory.co.uk in 2005, we offered PayPal and WorldPay as methods of payment. WorldPay turned out to be expensive, so we swapped it for Nochex, reducing our costs while offering similar facilities.

One final note on payment: think very carefully about accepting payment by cheque. It's likely you'll attract extra orders that way, but our experience – through both PassYourTheory and eBay – has been that accepting cheques is more trouble than it's worth. A high percentage of orders are never paid for, and they take longer to process and require more administration work.

SETTING UP YOUR CART Install the WP e-Commerce plugin in the usual way (see p80). You should then hide all the pages created by the plugin. Go to Pages > Edit and you'll find a series of new entries: Products Page, Checkout, Transaction Results and Your Account. For each, click Quick Edit and tick Private Page to ensure that only you, not visitors, can see these pages during development.

You'll see a new section in the Dashboard called Products. Go to Settings and, under General Settings, enter your regional information.

1 PAYMASTER Click Payment Options. The easiest payment provider to get started with is PayPal. Anyone with a PayPal Business account can offer PayPal Payments Standard, and to get that working all you need is your PayPal address. Enter this here.

2 CHECKOUT PROCESS Under Checkout, ensure you include all the relevant fields. If you need an extra field (for example, to let customers add special requirements) you can add it at the bottom. The most important of the other tabs is Shipping Options. Under Shipping Modules, select one of the Internal Shipping Calculators options, float your mouse over an option until Edit appears and click it. More often than not you'll want to choose Weight, and you can then add Layers, which specify cost bands. Unfortunately, the weight is expressed in pounds (lbs), so you'll need to convert from the grams used by the Royal Mail when working out your postage rates.

3 ADD PRODUCTS Now click Categories under Products on the left. You must set up at least one category, and in most case you'll need lots. Categories make it easier for customers to browse your shop; not everyone likes to use search. You want to have multiple products per category, but not too many. It's also a sign of credibility if you have various categories.

It's now time to add your first product. Click Products > Products and complete the form. In the Stock Keeping Unit field, type in the stock code you want to use for the product. Write a complete description using the Rich Text Editor, making sure you include everything your potential buyer needs to know. Select the category it belongs to and add any search tags that make sense.

The remaining fields are obvious. Finally, upload your product images; the more the better. Customers need the online equivalent of picking up and trying the product and that, generally speaking, means plenty of photos.

4 TESTING You should add a test product, at a low price, that you can use to make sure it all works. Then see how your shop is shaping up by editing the Products page and clicking Preview. Make sure you thoroughly test the entire process before it goes live.

Nochex is an alternative payment-processing service that makes a useful addition to systems based on Google Checkout and PayPal.

3

4

"Think very carefully about accepting cheques. Many orders are never paid for, and they require more work to process."

PART 3 **Marketing**

Find new customers

Introduction to marketing

Marketing your product is more important than getting your website right; arguably, more important than getting the product itself right. It's essential that you set up an effective marketing campaign and keep working on it over time. The good news is that marketing isn't rocket science. In fact, it's mainly about common sense and testing. It's also great fun.

What is marketing? Well, it's more than just advertising, but exactly how it's defined depends on who you ask. Don't ask the Chartered Institute for Marketing, because the definition it gives encompasses just about everything. For an internet-based business, your focus is going to be mainly on direct marketing and, specifically, permission-based direct marketing.

At its most basic, marketing is the process by which you encourage the right customers to find and buy your products. In direct marketing, we do this by interacting with individuals who will then, we hope, buy our product direct from us. Contrast this with Coca-Cola, for example, whose marketing is all about supporting its brand and encouraging people to buy from retailers, who in turn buy their stock from Coca-Cola, thus passing on a proportion of their revenue. Coca-Cola doesn't have a one-to-one relationship with any of its consumers – and this is one way in which the internet, by contrast with traditional retail channels, can make it possible for you to interact more effectively with your customers than the big corporations.

"Permission-based" direct marketing is widely acknowledged as the most effective form of marketing for most internet businesses. As you might guess, this involves getting agreement from customers – and potential customers – to interact with them.

The main benefits of this approach are that your conversion rate increases hugely and that you can establish a relationship that leads to lots of sales over a long period. Indeed, many profitable internet products lose money on their initial sale, because their vendors will make it back over the longer term.

ATTRACTING TRAFFIC The first aim is to attract the right visitors to your site. Note the qualifier there: web traffic is of little use unless the people who visit your site are likely to buy. Indeed, one of the biggest mistakes amateur marketers make is to waste money attracting the wrong people. Get it right and you can find potential customers, either for free via the "organic" search listings or at the lowest possible cost via pay-per-click advertising.

Google's AdWords dominates the pay-per-click market. Get your campaigns right to reap greater profit per sale.

Aweber is one of the leading auto-responder providers, characterised by its simple wizard-based approach.

Once you have visitors arriving at your site, it's essential that you convert the maximum number of them into buyers. This is rarely done instantly, and most successful internet businesses seek to establish a relationship with their potential customers rather than sell to them immediately. This usually involves the visitor giving their email address and permission for you to contact them in exchange for something you provide to them for free.

The organic search results are those that appear in the main listing area of Google, Bing or Yahoo!. These listings are lifted from the database that's created as the search engine scans websites and categorises them according to their content. Appearing high up the listings for your most profitable keywords means you will get free traffic from people who have searched for relevant words and are therefore likely to be interested in your product.

THE JOY OF SEO The process of ensuring your site is as highly ranked as possible is known as search engine optimisation, or SEO. A great deal of mystique surrounds this, but there's a limited range of aspects of your site that you need to work on, and it's possible for the layman to grasp the essentials, despite the claims of some specialist companies.

The first thing to understand and accept is that there's no way of guaranteeing the top spot for any high-traffic keywords. Any SEO company that claims to be able to achieve this is either lying or will only guarantee the top position to a very limited, low-traffic key phrase. Avoid this kind of claim like the plague: there are plenty of reputable companies out there if you feel you need help. As with so many things, you can do most of the optimising yourself, for free – and, in fact, much of the optimisation has to be done by you in any case, whether you hire someone or not.

Second, you need to accept that SEO takes time. Google rewards sites for their longevity in two ways. First, it will rank an older site higher than an equivalent newer site. Second, you earn credit for the number of incoming links to your site (but only links from relevant, highly ranked sites), and these take time to accumulate.

The really good news is that using sensible "white hat" techniques to optimise your site will also improve its effectiveness when it comes to converting sales and make it cheaper to advertise using Google AdWords.

PAY-PER-CLICK ADVERTISING When most people think about internet marketing, they think about Google AdWords. While AdWords can't build a relationship with a client or sell a product directly, it can drive targeted, relevant traffic to your site at a price you set yourself.

The earliest forms of internet advertising were paid for per thousand impressions (PPM), whereas with

> "The first aim is to get the right visitors. Web traffic is of little use unless the people who visit your site are likely to buy."

pay per click (PPC) you pay only when a potential visitor clicks the ad and visits your site. Aside from that obvious advantage, this mechanism makes it possible to track the effectiveness of your ad by measuring its click-through rate (CTR), the percentage of those who view the ad that go on to click on it. You can then extend that to tracking the sales themselves, so that you can tell which ads end up with the most profit per sale.

Google stole a march on Yahoo! by introducing a much more sophisticated treatment of PPC, and offers by far the best service to advertisers as well as the biggest market share. In most cases the best technique is to get your ad campaign working effectively via AdWords and then export it to the Yahoo! and Microsoft equivalents.

PERMISSION MARKETING Once a user arrives at your site, you need to make sure you begin a long-term relationship with a profitable percentage. This means giving them something of worth in return for their contact details – usually no more than a name and email address. Over the following days, your customer will receive specially written emails with two purposes: to encourage them to read more emails and, ultimately, to make the sale. Not surprisingly, if you make every email a sales letter, your potential customer will read part of the first one and then unsubscribe.

This automated sequence of emails is called an "autoresponder". In my view, the autoresponder is the most powerful, and most poorly used, weapon in the internet marketer's arsenal. A good autoresponder sequence will convert a far higher percentage of customers than a simple sales page, while building a mutually beneficial long-term relationship that leads to more sales.

How to optimise your copy

Search engines reward "relevance" – how closely the content of a web page matches the search phrase typed in. Your aim is to ensure that the right page from your site appears as high as possible in the rankings. So sensible search engine optimisation (SEO) involves not only getting your content right, but also structuring it in such a way that the mechanised process that the search engines use results in the best possible indexing.

Search engines serve up a link to an entire page, so the page is the fundamental unit you need to think about. Broadly speaking, each page should deal with a single major content area. If you have a range of products, each should be on its own page. For example, the driving theory test comprises a multiple-choice test and a video simulation. To rank well, each needs to be on its own page: this way, the density of the relevant keywords on the page is much higher.

STRUCTURE Within each page, you need to structure your content to reinforce the main messages it contains. Google tends to give extra weighting to the top 25% and bottom 25% of copy on any page. When it comes to deciding if the page is relevant, keywords in those places outrank those in the middle. The lesson is to make sure your main, keyword-dense, messages are near the top and the bottom.

On most web pages, users tend to pay attention to the top of the page, then the bottom, and finally spend the least time on the middle. Google's weighting of the content is designed to mirror this behaviour – one of the

ways it succeeds over its competitors by providing the most relevant results. Since visitors look primarily at the top and foot of the page, they are more likely to regard the results of their search as relevant – and therefore continue to use Google – if they find their search terms here.

HTML TAGS Remember HTML is supposed to describe the *meaning* of the content, not how it *looks*. The <h1> ("Heading 1") tag is intended to indicate that this text is the most important on the page. Accordingly, Google gives greater weighting to <h1> text. So your main heading, being <h1>, needs to include your most important keywords. Don't, for example, write a clever or oblique heading that doesn't mention any of your keywords – or if you do, give it a different tag, using <h1> for a more direct piece of copy, even if your CSS then makes this visually less prominent. Google gives proportionate priority to the other headings, <h2> being higher than <h3> and so on. Structure your headings with this in mind, and make sure you have only one <h1> tag, fewer <h2> than <h3> tags and so on.

Within paragraphs, Google prioritises text contained within the <strong> and <em> tags. These usually appear as bold or italic, and Google assumes you think they're more important. There's a case, therefore, for surrounding your keywords with <strong> tags. Again, your CSS determines the visual effect – which could be none.

Keep in mind that Google is trying to second-guess what a human reader will see as the most important words. Google doesn't buy anything from you, so remember the main point of your copy is to talk to humans. Sensible use of tags will make the page more effective for humans and for Google; go overboard and you'll satisfy neither.

IMAGE LINKS Believe it or not, images also impact on SEO. Again, this goes together with making the page useful for humans. For example, the alt element of the <img> tag – a piece of text attached to an image – was originally used to

Clear, standards-compliant code is easily digested by search-engine spiders. That means you maximise your rankings in the resiults without paying a penny.

describe the image while it loaded. When that was no longer useful, many designers ignored it. But alt text is also used by screen-reader software to describe images to users who can't see them, and is essential for accessibility.

When Google's "spider" visits a page, every text element is read. It sees the text part of an <img> tag as text, so adding your keywords to an alt element will increase the page's keyword density. But this is worth doing only if you can preserve the real purpose of alt, to describe the image accurately. Less obviously, adding your keywords to the URL of the image will also increase keyword density at no cost. All you need to do is change the filenames of your images to include your keywords, inserting hyphens between the words. For example, here's the HTML for an image from a page covering the Hazard Perception test:

was first developed, it described the meaning of the page while including presentational tags such as <b> (bold) and <font> to give more – albeit primitive – design control. More than a decade ago, however, CSS was introduced to allow presentation to be handled outside the HTML, as we explained on pp48-53. Sadly, many people still use outdated presentational HTML to clog up their pages: I strongly advise you to avoid this mistake.

The biggest culprit is the use of tables for layout. The <table> tag was developed to allow the presentation of spreadsheet-style figures, but designers quickly found they could lay out entire pages using table cells. Table-based layouts often have tables nested within tables within tables.

This causes a number of problems. First, the page becomes absolute gobbledygook for screen readers and,

Turn off CSS and images (above left) and you get a good idea of how your site looks to a search-engine spider. Here, the main heading and first part of the copy contain our keywords. On the right is how a table-based site might look to Google. It's not nearly so obvious what this site is about or the relative importance of the keywords – assuming there are any.

"Google gives extra weighting to the top 25% and bottom 25% of a page. Keywords in those places outrank those in the middle."

```
<img src="/images/screenshot1.jpg"
alt="Test footage" />
```

And here it is after optimisation:

```
<img src="/images/hazard-perception-
example-screen.jpg"
alt="Hazard Perception example screen" />
```

The revised version includes the key phrase "hazard perception" twice, while also making it clearer what the image is about – good for both Google and your visitors.

STICKING TO STANDARDS Your website will be indexed much more effectively by search engines if you strictly separate content from presentation. When HTML

therefore, very hard for search-engine spiders to make sense of. Second, the sheer quantity of <table>,<td> and <tr> tags swamps the copy and messes up your attempts to manage the keyword density. Third, your site is unlikely to work on mobile devices. Finally, the site is almost impossible to redesign without changing every single page (a CSS-based site can be redesigned without touching the HTML). For all these reasons, my advice is to avoid presentational HTML entirely and use CSS for all your design.

An easy way to see how your site looks to Google is to disable CSS and images. For example, using the Web Developer toolbar in Firefox, go to CSS > Disable Styles > All Styles and Images > Disable Images > All Images. You can now check that your headings and other tags include your keywords and, crucially, whether your most important copy is at the top or bottom of the page, as seen by the spider.

Metadata and links

View the source code of any website (see p48) and you'll see, near the top, a series of "meta" tags. The purpose of these is to provide information about the page to search engines. As you might guess, this can be abused to tell search engines what you want them to believe, rather than the truth. But search engines have become more sophisticated, and now index pages based on their actual content, not the web designer's meta tags.

The long and the short of it is that meta tags have practically no impact on your search engine ranking. The most common meta tags are "Description", "Keywords", "Robots", "Generator" and "Revisit-After". The old technique was to stuff the "Keywords" tag with your chosen keywords, but today this is more likely to do harm than good. By all means put your main keywords in there, but don't expect any significant benefit, and don't try to pack hundreds in.

The only meta tag you should always include is "Description". While this doesn't improve your ranking, it does give you control over how your site appears in the search results. All major search engines use this tag as the text that appears beneath the site link. Google and Bing use the text on its own, whereas Yahoo! will pad it out with content from your site to fill the available space. In the absence of a Description meta tag, all search engines will grab some of the content of the page itself and present that instead. That gives you much less control over exactly what appears. Bear in mind that whatever keywords the searcher has typed in will appear in bold in the description section of the results, making your site appear more relevant and therefore more likely to be clicked.

Here's an example from PassYourTheory.co.uk:

<meta name="Description" content="The best Hazard Perception and Theory Test training anywhere. Official DSA Theory Test question bank and Hazard Perception video clips">

This text is used by Bing as our site description in the search results (Google takes exactly the same approach):

THE TITLE TAG While the meta tags have next to no impact on your ranking, it's essential to get the <title> tag right. This tag is placed in the <head> section alongside the meta tags, and has two effects. First, whatever you type here will appear in the browser title bar. More importantly, search engines use the contents of the title tag as the title of your listing. Including your main keywords in your title tag

The meta and title tags of a search engine optimisation (SEO) company – after all, they should know. It's essential to get the title and meta "Description" tags right to optimise your listing.

will boost your natural ranking – but take care, as always, to ensure that the title makes sense to humans, too.

INCOMING LINKS Search engines, particularly Google, rank results on three main criteria. The first is *relevance*. As we've said, this is mainly about getting your content to match the search phrases used by your potential customers. The details of the Google algorithm are a closely guarded and ever-evolving secret, but the search giant makes no secret of the fact that, along with relevance, two other factors are highly important. The first of these is *age*: longer-established sites tend to appear higher up the listings. The second is the number and, especially, the quality of *links* on the site.

By acquiring links from other relevant sites, you will improve your ranking considerably. You may have heard of PageRank. This is an algorithm invented by Google co-founder Larry Page to indicate the relative importance of a web page by analysing its links. It results in a number out of ten, which you can see if you download the Google Toolbar. Any incoming link from a site with a higher PageRank than yours will boost your position in the natural search listings as well as increasing your PageRank.

As an example, the BBC home page (www.bbc.co.uk) has a PageRank of 9/10 and is, therefore, considered by Google to be a leading authority. If (by some miracle) you could convince the BBC to link one if its relevant pages to your site – which almost certainly has a much lower PageRank – then that would boost your ranking. On the other hand, if you have a PageRank of 5 and your links are coming from sites with lower PageRanks, that will not have a positive effect on your listing position.

So the aim should be to get incoming links from authoritative sites. You could do this by providing free information of interest to their visitors, offering them discounts, or indeed paying the site for a link. A number of SEO companies offer to submit your site to hundreds of directories in return for a sizeable fee, but the value of these services is debatable.

You should certainly submit your site to the DMOZ directory (www.dmoz.org), as it's well recognised and used by major search engines. Other directories should be chosen with care: make sure they're relevant and have a greater PageRank than you.

OUTGOING LINKS If you have owned a website for any length of time, you've probably received emails asking to exchange links. In other words, the emailer offers to add a link to your site in return for you adding a link to theirs. There's some debate about the effect that outgoing links have on your PageRank, but it seems likely

> **"Meta tags now have practically no impact on your SEO. By all means put your main keywords in, but don't expect any significant benefit."**

Do you find these tags informative, or are they just clutter? Modern search engines feel much the same way about superfluous metadata in web pages.

that outgoing links will have either no affect or a minor negative impact. As with all other matters SEO, it comes down to striking a balance between what's good for your ranking and what's good for your visitors. If you're offered a link exchange by a site with a higher PageRank than you, then generally speaking you should accept it as long as the outgoing link is likely to be of interest to your visitors.

All outgoing links should be set to launch in their own browser tab. To do this, use the following format:

```
<a href="http://www.thewebsite.com" target="_blank">My link text </a>
```

This is one of the few occasions when I think it's fine to disobey the XHTML 1.0 Strict guidelines, under which the target attribute is deprecated. What this HTML does is to launch the other site in its own window or tab (depending on how the user's browser is set up) rather than overwriting your site in the same window; after all, they might want to come back, and you need to make that as easy as possible.

How much time you spend on link building depends on the importance to you of appearing high in the organic rankings (as opposed to the paid-for "sponsored results"). Yet no matter how hard you work, achieving a high position in the organic rankings will take months or even years. For most new businesses this is simply too long, and they'll focus mainly on pay-per-click (PPC) advertising.

Given that you only have so many hours in the day, it makes sense to get your content as well-optimised as you can, submit yourself to the main search engines and directories, and then focus on your PPC campaign.

Using Google Analytics

Information is power: you need to know which pages on your site are popular, and track your visitors all the way from arriving at your site to clicking "Buy". Google Analytics does this for free.

This data can help you test and improve every step of the process. If, for example, a high number of users exit your site at a particular page, you can change it and see if it improves. Analytics will tell you where your visitors come from, whether via a pay-per-click ad, organic search results, links from other sites or typing your URL into a browser. This tells you which are the most important sources of traffic and which are most effective.

Analytics will also tell you about the browsers your visitors are using, whether they have plugins such as Flash Player, what languages they speak, whether they're a new or returning visitor and plenty more besides.

1 **SET UP YOUR ACCOUNT** To set up Google Analytics for a WordPress site, all you need is a free Google account. Armed with this, go to http://analytics.google.com and click Sign Up. You'll find yourself at the New Account Signup page. Enter your site's URL where requested, give it a name and set your location.

2 **GET TRACKING** Click Continue and fill in your contact details. Click Continue again, read

the Terms and Conditions and click Yes. Click Create New Account. You're presented with your tracking code. Be sure to use the "New Tracking Code". This JavaScript needs to be inserted into every page on your site. Here's how to do it in WordPress. Run FileZilla and navigate to the /wp-content/themes/theme-name/ folder. You need to find a file called "footer.php" which, as its name suggests, creates the footer for every page. Copy this file to your hard disk.

3 **EDIT YOUR FOOTER** Open the file in PSPad or Notepad. Find the entry "<?php wp_footer(); ?>". Switch back to the Analytics page and click on the tracking code. This should select it; now right-click and select Copy. Paste the code after the above line in the footer.php file. Use FileZilla to upload footer.php back to its original location. Click Finish to complete the setup.

4 **FINAL CHECKS** Make sure the tracking code is working. From the Analytics Overview, click Edit next to your domain name. You'll see "Tracking Unknown" at the top right. Click the Check Status link to force Analytics to analyse the page. It should confirm that you're all set. Come back in a day or two to see some stats.

1

2

3

4

Beginner's guide to keywords

Keywords help search engines determine if your web pages are relevant to the search terms entered by a user. However, making your pages more relevant is not simply a matter of packing your copy with your chosen keywords. In the early days of search engines this was accepted practice, but now you're much more likely to see your site punished for this rather than rewarded.

Why? Well, search engines such as Google, Yahoo and Bing compete largely on the quality of the results that users get. Google dominates the market because of its obsession with presenting the most relevant search results, and it continues to focus on this as its number one priority. If a page is artificially padded out with keywords it will irritate the visitor and probably result in them clicking the Back button – not the result either you or Google was looking for.

Here's how to assess your keywords properly.

1 **LOAD THE TOOL** Google should be your first target when optimising your site, so start with its keyword tool. Go to www.google.co.uk/sktool to load the Search-based Keyword Tool. In the Website field, type the URL of one of your main competitors, then click Find Keywords.

2 **FIRST RESULTS** This will present a list of keywords, ranked by the number of searches carried out per month on each. This search figure is surprisingly inaccurate in my experience, but it does give a rough indication of the relative importance of each. You can also see the price that Google suggests you bid for the keyword when setting up your AdWords (see p102). You can ignore this figure, but it does show which keywords are more expensive.

Finally, you'll see a graphical indication of the level of competition for that keyword. Pay particular attention to high-volume keywords with low to moderate completion.

You can use the Export button to export these keywords as a CSV file, which you can later paste into your AdWords campaign.

3 **FIND THE KEY** Bear in mind that your rivals may be poor at optimising their sites, and their product range may be different to yours, so this isn't a complete list. But it does offer a start. Looking at the list for my candle-making site, I can immediately discount some of these keywords as I won't be stocking those products; I'll also

be adding my most important key phrase, "candle making kits", which this competitor doesn't stock.

4 **KEY PHRASES** At this stage, don't bother with keywords that have a low number of monthly searches. I've drawn the line at 500, and most of my effort will be focused on high-traffic keywords. Equally, avoid very generic keywords that have massive monthly traffic: while this won't cost you anything financially, it signals huge competition and makes it much harder to rank near the top. In most cases, your keywords will actually be phrases. For example, with www.makingyourowncandles.co.uk I won't be focusing specifically on "candle" or "candles", but rather on "candle making" and "candle making kit". Both of these contain "candle" too, and so will rank against that keyword, but I don't expect a high position.

Finally, remember to include the word "buy" alongside your product names in your copy where possible, as many searchers will type "buy candle" rather than just "candle". Similarly, if your product is seasonal, include "Christmas" or "summer" in your copy alongside it.

Get blogging!

In this book I've advocated using WordPress to create your business website. As you may know, WordPress was originally developed as a blogging platform, so it's worth thinking about using it for that purpose, too. There are two basic approaches to blogging: publishing under your own name, to express your personal views and perhaps connect with friends and colleagues, and blogging under the identity of your business.

These days the blog as personal web diary is increasingly being replaced by Facebook and Twitter, and for most users is unlikely to achieve anything much from a commercial point of view. Unless you're a celebrity, it's probably much more effective to create a blog under the name of your business rather than your personal identity. WordPress makes it simple to mix blog posts and web pages in the same site, so you can integrate your company blog with your main sales website.

WHAT'S THE POINT? As a businessperson, you'll want your blog, like everything else you spend time on, to have a specific business function that contributes to your bottom line; if you feel the need to vent your spleen on any particular topics, a personal blog is the way to go. Having said that, don't make the mistake of thinking you need to be balanced and neutral with all your company blog entries. Your aim is to have people return on a regular basis or subscribe to your blog, and nothing is more likely to put people off than a bland, corporate-style blog. The key is to keep it on-topic and avoid any really outrageous views that might alienate customers.

To contribute to your profitability, your blog must either make it more likely that your customers will buy your company's products or it must make money for itself.

BRINGING IN CUSTOMERS A well-written, relevant blog will help establish a relationship of trust with potential customers, which can then lead to sales. A blog of this sort establishes you as a figure of authority in your market and the natural choice for the customer. If you've based your business on your interests and expertise, creating a credible, useful blog shouldn't be difficult – but it does take time.

My top seven tips for a successful business blog:

1 Know your audience

In developing your product, you will have defined who is your typical customer. Every blog entry you consider writing should be relevant and interesting to this target audience. You should always be writing to that individual, using a voice that suits and appeals to them.

Posterous makes it easy to update your blog and social networks.

Glenn Livingston's blog has great content to entice you to sign up.

2 Write with personality

Think about the personality you want to project in your blog. It's unlikely to be "boring, middle-aged corporate-speak". Look at some of the best business blogs (see right) and analyse how the way in which they've been written affects how you perceive them and their company. You can also find inspiration in magazines and books that appeal to your target audience.

3 Write what's interesting

Nobody will read a boring blog. Come up with interesting angles or be the first with news or opinions. If you solve a problem that's relevant to your customers, blog about it. Whatever you do, don't start a blog that is nothing more than a list of links to other blogs.

4 Link it to your business

A common mistake is to expect visitors to understand how your blog relates to your business. Most people don't want to think that hard. Make it clear who you are and what your business does. Include obvious links to the business.

5 Capture their details

Blogs should be open to all visitors; it's not a good idea to require them to register to view your posts, unless there's intrinsic value in the information or resources on the protected pages. By writing an eBook, recording an interview or buying resale rights to useful resources, you can offer the visitor something in exchange for their details. Once you have these, you can begin to establish a longer-term relationship that might lead to multiple sales.

6 Keep updating

How many blogs have you come across that look interesting on the face of it, until you notice that they were last updated months or even years ago? An outdated blog is worse than no blog at all. Services such as Posterous (www.posterous.com) make it easy to update your blog, Twitter feed and Facebook page via email. There's no excuse.

Best blogs

If you want to see how it's done, these are some of my favourite business blogs.

www.perrymarshall.com
Combined blog and website of the foremost AdWords and internet-marketing expert.

www.payperclick searchmarketing.com
Glenn Livingston's pay-per-click marketing blog: full of excellent material, and a good example of how to get someone to begin a relationship by offering something valuable. (Also notice the shining example of a keyword-filled URL!)

www.alistapart.com
A List Apart is an excellent and long-established blog aimed at web developers.

www.smashing magazine.com
Smashing magazine's blog is specifically for web designers.

www.pcpro.co.uk/blogs
Naturally, the best technology blog!

7 Host it yourself

Don't use free hosted services such as WordPress.com or Blogspot.com. Like using a Hotmail address for your business, this suggests you're a cheapskate or incompetent.

HOW TO BLOG FOR MONEY First, build an audience. The more relevant people who visit you, the more sales you'll make from your main business and the more potential there will be to make money from the blog itself. Once you've built your blog and populated it with useful articles, you can then drive traffic to it using the SEO techniques we've covered and a low-cost Google AdWords campaign.

You can make money directly from a healthy blog by selling advertising space or selling products as an affiliate. Ads are very simple to set up, especially if you use Google AdSense, but unless you have a massive audience, they'll generate only a small income. On the other hand, many bloggers have built entire businesses around affiliate marketing, not least because of the low setup cost.

Keep in mind that you are creating a blog that people want to revisit and recommend. Making money from advertising or affiliate schemes depends on having a viable blog in the first place. This is increasingly important, as Google appears to be preparing to eliminate blogs that only "review" products for which the blog owner is an affiliate.

If you want to add affiliate products to your site, these are my recommendations:

 DON'T OVERDO IT Make sure no more than 10-20% of posts link to an affiliate product. This will prevent it feeling like a pure sales page.

 BUY THE PRODUCTS There's no excuse for selling a product you haven't personally used. By buying and using a product you will see how it works and be able to write a balanced review (it's essential to include cons as well as pros). This will also ensure you don't recommend duff products to your audience, which will alienate them and could result in costly returns.

STAY RELEVANT Stick to products that are truly relevant to your audience. Your blog will only succeed if it is focused, and your credibility only counts in the areas in which you've built that credibility.

Relationship-based marketing

Would you buy from a stranger? Probably not – yet many web businesses are based on exactly that premise. Create (or buy in) a product, add a shopping cart, run a pay-per-click ad, then sit back and watch the lucre roll in. Or not. Even if customers do buy, most businesses then forget about them. You can do better.

Businesses that don't build customer relationships can make money only if every transaction is profitable. The costs of production, running your business and marketing must add up to less than the price customers pay for an item. This is increasingly hard to achieve as the cost of pay-per-click (PPC) advertising rises, and it's not how successful bricks-and-mortar businesses work. A Tesco Clubcard, for example, is the basis of a long-term relationship with the supermarket that encourages you to shop there. Even your local car mechanic has the advantage of a roadside location and passing traffic. An internet site, unless brilliantly optimised to appear on Google's first page or have a wide network of incoming links, is invisible unless you're running a PPC campaign, and if you are, every click is costing you money.

The internet also suffers from a lack of trust. If I go into my local corner shop, however run-down it is, I know I'll be able to take the contents of my shopping basket home once I've paid. This isn't the case online, so your customers are understandably concerned about handing over their credit-card details to a company they don't know.

This contributes to the low conversion rates of most websites. A website is doing well if it achieves 2%

conversion; many languish at below 1%. Think about that: over 98 out of every 100 visitors – who have arrived at your site by clicking on an advert targeted at them – *do not buy*. If you're spending 10p per click and getting a 2% conversion rate, each conversion is costing you around £5. In practice the figure can be much worse, and many, many new web businesses fail because they can't make PPC pay.

Traditionally, marketing has relied almost entirely on "interruption advertising". TV and radio adverts are typical examples of that; they rely on interrupting your chain of thought, making an impression, getting across a message and having you take some sort of action. In the 1950s and 1960s this approach worked because there were few channels through which to advertise, but these days we're all exposed to hundreds of interruptions per day.

Instead, as we saw on p86, successful internet and direct marketing is usually permission marketing. Under this model, potential customers are attracted to your site by interruption advertising, links or recommendation, but then enter into a mutually beneficial long-term relationship with you. Usually, this begins with you offering something worthwhile in exchange for your visitor's name and email address.

Seth Godin literally wrote the book on this subject. *Permission Marketing: Turning Strangers into Friends and Friends into Customers* (£7.49 from www.amazon.co.uk) is still a bestseller despite being more than ten years old. Godin's blog (http://sethgodin.typepad.com) is also worth reading for advice and analysis.

And for the doubters

I appreciate that many people are suspicious of the internet. Some people will believe that we made up all the testimonials you see around the site or that everything on the internet is a scam. Well, there's not much I can do about that but if you just need a little more convincing then please sign up for our FREE trial membership. This gives you the opportunity to try 3 FREE, fully functional mock theory tests with absolutely no obligation to buy anything.

You'll see how useful and realistic our theory test is before you commit to becoming a member. Add that to our pass pledge (if you become a Premier Member and then fail we will refund your membership twice over!) and our outstanding track record and you've got nothing to lose!

First name & Surname

Your E-Mail :

[Sign Me Up For a FREE Trial Membership]

Consumers are quite guarded about giving away their email addresses – perhaps increasingly so. You must offer something of value to persuade them.

"Traditional marketing relies on interruption advertising. These days we're exposed to hundreds of interruptions per day."

The potential customer is then sent a series of emails, written by you (if you're tempted to buy them in, you're missing the point), at pre-programmed intervals. The ultimate aim of these, of course, is to make one or more sales, but they should be mainly devoted to providing great information to your subscriber.

The key is to ensure your emails are anticipated by people who have volunteered to receive information from you. Your emails are then not junk or spam, but a welcome source of knowledge (and maybe, if you're a good writer, even entertainment). This means the permission you've purchased with your initial freebie needs to be renewed with each and every message. Abuse that trust just once, and your carefully cultivated relationship can be ended instantly.

That's not to say you shouldn't use your auto-responder sequence to sell your product or service. Rather, the sales pitch needs to be relevant to the subject matter and must occupy a relatively small portion of the message. A good rule of thumb is that 80% of your message should be useful, free information, which buys you the right to spend 20% of the message selling. This might be 20% of a single email, or one sales message out of every five emails.

GETTING THE DEAL RIGHT The biggest single impediment to a successful autoresponder campaign is the site owner's reluctance to give away too much free of charge. If you don't give away something of true value, potential customers won't sign up in sufficient numbers. Let's imagine you're selling aquarium accessories. Your job is to establish your credibility as a trustworthy figure of authority. You may well have set up a blog (see p94), and your autoresponder will reinforce this while giving you the opportunity to sell to the customer.

Algae is a common problem for owners of fish tanks, and among your various product lines you sell anti-algae tablets and gizmos. The email your customers want to receive (especially if they've responded to a PPC ad that mentions solving algae problems) is one that tells them how to prevent algae forming in their tank. But hold on: doesn't that mean they won't buy your anti-algae tabs? Perhaps. If they follow your tips, they won't need your tabs – but they'll almost certainly need some other accessories, and who are they going to buy them from? That helpful person with the anti-algae advice.

By giving something authoritative away for free, you make these people much more likely to buy from you later, particularly if you send a whole sequence of useful emails to them. And thanks to human nature (and laziness), many of your customers won't actually follow your advice on clearing the algae because it's too much like hard work, and will buy anti-algae tablets from you in any case, since your emails show you know what you're talking about.

Autoresponders are the classic quid pro quo: everyone wins. You end up with a long-term, well-informed customer whose multiple purchases outweigh the original cost of attracting them; and your customer ends up with a trusted supplier of the things they genuinely need. ➜

Even when you're selling something that, by its nature, people might need only once – such as advice for a driving test – you can increase your profitability by building ongoing relationships.

Case study
PassYourTheory.co.uk

PassYourTheory.co.uk has a fundamental problem: drivers need to pass their test only once. It might seem, therefore, that we need to make a sale on the user's first visit. In fact, it's hard to make a profit that way, so we use autoresponders to increase our conversion rate.

Think about the way you search for a product. Typically, you'll type a search term into Google, then visit a number of the sites that appear both in the Sponsored Listings and the organic results. Very often you'll want to mull it over before buying, and unless you're very organised, by the time you come back, credit card in hand, you've forgotten which one you liked best. Alternatively, you leave it for a week or two and whatever inspired you to search in the first place has been long forgotten.

Now imagine what would happen if one of those sites you visited emailed you a couple of days later with an informative email and a link to their sign-up pages. Wouldn't you be more likely simply to click the link and buy from them rather than start again?

This is the approach we use at PassYourTheory. If we can't get the visitor to buy on the spot, we offer them a free trial membership; as part of that, they get a sequence of emails starting two days later. These contain sample theory questions along with answers and hints and tips. At the end of each email is a reminder to sign up for our full service. All of this is entirely automated.

Used like this, autoresponders can make the difference between your site making a loss and a healthy profit.

STEP BY STEP Set up an autoresponder

1 **SIGN UP** Go to www.aweber.com and click Order. I would always sign up for month-by-month membership in case I don't get on with a service. Complete your details, sign up and click Let's Get Started. You can now create a "double opt-in" email.

2 **FIRST EMAIL** Current anti-spam regulations require that anyone signing up to your email list confirms their request by clicking a link in an email. The first email you create will encourage them to click the verification link. Note here that I'm using the field {!firstname_fix}. This inserts the user's first name – they will have supplied this on registering – and the "fix" part means it'll automatically capitalise the first letter if they didn't. So, if sent to me, the email would have a subject line: "Kevin, Confirm your subscription".

Some internet marketers believe that adding the user's name to the subject line makes it more likely they'll open the email, but the only way to know is to test it. In my view it does no harm if not overused. The "Confirmation Success Page" is the page on your site that subscribers are directed to once they've verified. This is optional, but a very good idea. If you're using WordPress, create a page specifically for the purpose and enter its URL here.

You can now go on to edit your first email, which subscribers will receive on completing the verification process. You have the choice of sending in HTML or plain-text format (or both). I recommend plain text, as it's much more likely to make it through your users' junk filters, and HTML in email clients is unpredictable.

3 **CREATE A WEB FORM** You can now create a web form that will be used by subscribers to sign up. I strongly recommend the "In-line" format, which creates some code for you to insert in your site with a standard pair of input fields for the user's name and email address. Avoid any form of pop-up or pop-under, as visitors often loathe them.

You can specify a "thank you" page that will tell users to check their email for the verification message. You can also forward variables to the thank you page, which makes it possible, with a bit of coding, to capture succscribers' details and add them to your own database. If, for example, you give away access to specific parts of your site, or a download, then you could have AWeber send the customer's email address and name to your website to facilitate this. Scroll down to the bottom of the page and click Get HTML. This should be copied into your page or post (use the HTML view in WordPress).

4 **NEW MESSAGES** You can now go through the process of adding further messages. Remember, it's your job to encourage your subscribers to read the next message in the sequence. Your emails must be anticipated and welcomed by your subscribers, and this means including genuinely useful information with the minimum of sales pitch. If you want to see a superb autoresponder sequence, go to www.perrymarshall.com and complete the form to receive "5 Days to Success with Google AdWords". This will give you an idea of how to structure your own sequences.

Search engines: how to get listed

Any site containing inbound links will eventually be indexed by all the major search engines, but you can submit it manually to be sure.

Yahoo still offers a £199 service to speed up adding your site, but with Google and Bing you can manually submit it free. Google currently represents around 80% of total search traffic, so make sure your site is set up properly for it first.

1 **ADD YOUR SITE** Go to www.google.com/webmasters/tools, click the "Add a site..." button and type in the URL of your site. Click Continue and you'll be presented with a verification screen: this is there to ensure you own the site. In FileZilla, go to your /wp-content/themes/theme-name folder, find header.php and copy it over to your PC.

2 **META TAG** Open the header.php file in PSPad (or Notepad) and copy the <meta> tag from Google Tools into the <head> section. Save it and copy it back to the server, overwriting the existing file. Click Verify and, all being well, you'll be taken to your dashboard. There won't be much to see, since the site won't yet have been visited by the spider. In the meantime, you should create a sitemap to help the search engines index your site

properly. A sitemap is an XML file in a standard format; WordPress has a free plugin to create it automatically. From Plugins in your WordPress Dashboard, search for "Google XML Sitemaps". Click Install.

3 **SUBMIT SITEMAP** Go to Settings > XML-Sitemap. Ignore all the options for now. Hit "Click here" at the top to build your map. Then make sure Google has found it: in the Google Webmaster Tools dashboard, click Site Configuration > Sitemaps, click Submit a Sitemap, type "sitemap.xml" and click Submit Sitemap. The sitemap.xml file also works with Bing: find its equivalent tools at www.bing.com/webmaster.

4 **CHECK KEYWORDS** Once the Google spider has visited, you'll see a range of data that complements Google Analytics (p92). For example, it shows how Google sees your site, where incoming links are from, the top search queries and where you appeared in the organic listings. Note the summary of keywords found across the site; check the top ones are your most important.

Getting your keywords right

There's nothing more important to the success of an AdWords campaign than finding the right keywords: they determine who will see your ad. There's clearly no point in having your ad displayed to the wrong people, since that will result in the twin nightmares of low click-through rate and low conversion rate.

The greatest problems come when you focus on keywords that are close to the correct ones but don't attract buyers. For example, imagine you sell candle-making kits, like our example business. If you decide your ads will target searchers who type "candles", you're making an expensive mistake: they may be looking purely for information, or to buy ready-made candles. Maybe a few of them are looking for kits, but the percentage will be tiny, with the result that your click-through will be very low and your conversion even lower. The people seeing your ad are casual browsers, not buyers. And remember, if by chance they do click your ad, but don't buy anything, they've cost you money.

Contrast this with using the key phrase "candle making". A searcher who types this is likely to be looking for information on candle making or a supplier of candle-making materials. This keyword might well be profitable.

Even better, having "candle making kit" as your main key phrase would be much more likely to attract active buyers.

CHOOSE YOUR WORDS WISELY It's essential to start your campaign with a small set of highly focused keywords. Many AdWords "gurus" will encourage you to generate a list of dozens (or even hundreds) of "long tail" keywords that each generate only a small amount of traffic but have little competition. However, doing this from the beginning only serves to cloud the issue. In most AdWords campaigns, the vast majority of profitable clicks come from a small percentage of your keywords.

An 80/20 rule is often cited: 80% of your clicks will come from 20% of your keywords. If you follow that through, you'll see that, in fact, 65% of your clicks come from around 4% of your keywords (20% of the 20%). Of

> **"Imagine you sell candle-making kits. If you decide to target searchers who type 'candles', you're making an expensive mistake."**

Enter a key phrase to see Google's analysis of related keywords.

Click the Add link beside each keyword you want to pursue.

Create multiple Ad Groups for different sets of relevant keywords.

course, the actual figures will vary, but the fact remains that it makes sense to work on the most productive keywords rather than getting carried away with the long tail – the additional ones that might generate a few extra sales.

Begin with your primary keywords: the ones you've used for your company name, domain name, blog title and SEO. For example, with PassYourTheory.co.uk the primary key phrase is "theory test"; for MakingYourOwn Candles.co.uk, it's "candle-making kits"; and for Greeting CardMaker it's "card making". Remember that in part 1 of this guide we established that there was probably sufficient volume in the market for those keywords. Throughout this process, check that each keyword or phrase is aimed squarely at your intended customer: it's easy to get drawn into irrelevant keywords because of the number on offer.

FIND GOOGLE KEYWORDS Go to https://AdWords. google.co.uk/select/KeywordToolExternal and type your primary keyword phrase into the box (see opposite, bottom left). Make sure "Use synonyms" is checked and sort the results by "Local Search Volume" (if you're targeting the UK). Under "Show/hide columns", select "Estimated Avg. CPC".

You'll now see a list containing your term and all the terms that Google thinks are related to your primary keyword phrase. You'll also see the search volume and a bar showing the level of Advertiser Competition. Finally, you'll see Google's estimate of the cost of an ad based on that keyword appearing in one of the top three positions.

Take this estimate with a shovel full of salt: Google can't take relevance into account since you haven't, at this point, told it which domain the ad will be linked to, or the ad text. In my experience, the estimated average cost per click can be out by a factor of five or more. Also bear in mind that it's an average. In most markets, the ads in positions 1 and 2 might be disproportionately expensive compared to 3 and 4, so the average is skewed. I've seen examples where the Google estimate was 75p but the actual cost for position 3 was 13p.

What's the point, then? Well, the estimate is a good indicator of the relative cost of each keyword phrase. You can see that our main phrase, "card making", has an estimated average CPC of 65p, whereas the similar "make cards" is predicted to be nearly twice as expensive. You'll also notice that the top few keywords account for a huge proportion of the potential traffic, so we'll concentrate on those for now.

FOCUS YOUR CHOICES You now need to go through the list and click the Add link next to your primary keyword and those that are closely related and likely to cost a similar amount. In this example, I've chosen "card making", "cards making", "making a card" and "card making uk" since they

are essentially interchangeable. Why not "card making kits" or "card making ideas"? Because searchers typing those keywords into Google are not necessarily looking for the same as those typing "card making", and it's essential to keep your ads focused. You now have your first Ad Group.

AD GROUPS The next step is to find one or more additional Ad Groups based on different sets of keywords. An excellent way of doing this is to analyse what your competitors are advertising against. Click the "Website content" radio button at the top and type in the URL of your main competitor. Google will then trawl its site looking for relevant keywords. Again, list them by local search volume. You need to be careful here if your product is significantly different from the competition (as it should be) and only pick keywords that are relevant to *your* product.

Google helpfully categorises the keywords, and I'm drawn immediately to "greeting cards". This is obviously closely tied to "card making", except that it's too wide: lots of people searching on that phrase will be looking to buy pre-printed cards. So we're looking for phrases that qualify our customer better. In this case I'm adding "handmade greeting cards", "personalised greeting cards", "blank greeting cards" and "alternative greeting cards" to my list, because in each case the keywords suggest the user wants to customise their card. Some other alternatives, such as "photo greeting cards", have been rejected at this stage because their cost per click is very high.

So these are the keywords for my next Ad Group. Looking down the list, I see keywords related to birthday cards, so I'll also create an Ad Group based on those words.

After all this, you should end up with three to six groups of keywords with between one and six highly focused keywords or phrases in each. My advice is to take your time over this: choosing the right initial keywords will give your AdWords campaign the best possible start. It's then a matter of testing, refining and expanding over time.

Don't look now...

It may well be that there are certain combinations of keywords that you specifically don't want to result in visits to your website. The classic example of this, when you're running a commercial site, is any combination including "free". Searchers who specifically type "free" are relatively unlikely to pay for a product, however persuasive you may be. In these situations, you can specify that any search containing certain keywords should not result in your ad showing. Since every click incurs a cost, the use of negative keywords can be crucial in making your campaign profitable.

Introducing pay-per-click

Print advertising has been the mainstay of the marketing of businesses – large and small – for over a century. For a small firm, it might be an ad in a local paper or the Yellow Pages. But each of these needs to interrupt the reader's flow, grab their attention and get them to buy. This is a lot to attempt in a tiny classified ad that can't be changed until the next reprint and that you pay for up front, whether or not anyone responds.

Pay-per-click (PPC) solves these problems. First, your ad appears when, and only when, a web user types in a word or phrase that's relevant to your product or service. This means the right people are more likely to see your ad. Second, you can amend the ad as much as you like and, indeed, run alternatives alongside each other to test which generates the most profit. Third, you only pay when the user actually clicks; if you get no clicks, you pay nothing.

PPC originated with Goto.com in 1998. Goto later metamorphosed into Overture and then became part of Yahoo, so you might expect Yahoo to be the main force in PPC, but today Google dominates the market with its AdWords programme – which, although it was introduced four years later than Goto.com, accounts for around 80% of the total global "paid search" market share.

The reason for this is linked to Google's success as a search engine. Right from the beginning, Google has focused on the importance of relevance in its search results. Web users quickly gravitated to Google when they started getting more useful results than with Yahoo or MSN.

Google applies this principle to its paid advertising, too. With Yahoo and Microsoft adCenter, the more you bid for your clicks, the higher in the paid results listing you'll appear. It's a bit like traditional advertising, where you'd pay for a better position in the hope – but with no guarantee – of a better response.

With Google, the bid price accounts for only around half of the ranking algorithm. Google also assesses how relevant your ad is to the searcher by examining the ad and its associated website and giving it a "Quality Score". The net result of this is that the more relevant ads will tend to appear higher up (good for the searcher) while also making it possible for focused, content-rich sites with well-written ads to outperform competitors who can afford to pay more per click.

Because of this advantage, we'll spend the next few pages focusing on Google's AdWords system. AdWords not only works better for startup businesses, it also offers the most sophisticated range of tools and reports to help make your campaign a success. So the best approach is

Type "learn about adwords" into Google and you get three full pages of ads by AdWords experts. It's an ideal way to see what's working right now.

Microsoft's Bing search engine tends to deliver fewer targeted ads than Google, as I found when I searched for the same phrase and got only four relevant sponsored links. Bing has only around 10% of the market, but the lack of competition could be an opportunity.

Refining your keywords and ad copy should be a never-ending cycle. With Google's sophisticated data available for free at all times, you'd be crazy not to base your business on solid analysis.

to get everything set up and profitable on Google before expanding into the other PPC systems.

ONE CAMPAIGN, THREE AUDIENCES An advertising campaign is made up of one or more Ad Groups, each of which is made up of one or more PPC ads triggered by a specific set of keywords and phrases. The ads themselves can be displayed in three places: within the Google search results (in the "Sponsored Links" down the right-hand side); within the search results of Google's partners, including Virgin Media and other Google entities such as Google Maps and Google Groups; and in the "Content Network".

The Content Network is made up of all websites signed up to Google's AdSense program, along with bigger

---

> **"Google AdWords not only works better, it also has the most sophisticated tools to help make your campaign a success."**

---

advertisers such as newspaper and media sites. Your Google Ads can be shown within this network, but in that context they function more like traditional interruption ads, since the web user is likely to be in "browse" rather than "buy" mode. As a general rule, you need to get your search campaign (Google and its Search Partners) working profitably before tackling the Content Network.

THE PROCESS The PPC process begins and ends with keyword research. In part 1 of this book we established your primary keyword phrase, derived from your company's one-sentence "elevator pitch". This phrase can be used in naming your business, its domain and its website title. It should also appear throughout your site. So your keyword research will begin centred on your primary keyword phrase and

DIY

If, despite my reassurances, you think all this sounds too much like hard work, what about outsourcing your AdWords management? As a rule, I don't recommend it. No-one knows your business (or cares about it) like you, so you're ideally placed to run your campaigns. There are only two situations where external management might be a good idea. First, if you really believe you have too little time. This will be rare, given that marketing is probably your most important activity. Second, once your campaign is up and running profitably, there might be a case for passing the day-to-day chores to someone else. For most of us, however, getting down and dirty with AdWords is an essential skill.

then move outwards, rather than simply picking up every related keyword regardless. Once you've come up with a list of keywords, these need to be split into related groups. Each of these clumps becomes an Ad Group in your AdWords Campaign. You'll create at least two ads within each group.

Typically, you might have three to six Ad Groups in your main campaign, so that's around 12 ads, each being shown to its own set of keywords. You activate the campaign and let it run for long enough to get conversion statistics that can be relied on: usually at least 100 clicks per ad. Then you can compare the performance of the Ad Groups against each other: how profitable is each? Are any burning money?

Within each Ad Group, you'll check the performance of your two (or more) ads, looking at the click-through rate (CTR; the percentage of people who click on the ad) and the conversion rate. This latter figure represents the percentage of people who arrive on your site and then go on to take whatever action you've specified – usually signing up to an email sequence or buying something. This is the key ratio; CTR is money down the drain if you're not converting.

You'll usually find one of the two ads in a group works substantially better. So you'll disable the poor performer, duplicate the winner and alter it in some way so you again have two ads running against each other. Also look at the keywords – Google tells you how each performs – and disable or delete those that are losing you money.

This continues ad infinitum. Initially you will probably see big performance gains in each cycle as you implement improvements, but these will tail off over time, at which point you'll enjoy consistent performance and can concentrate more on other aspects of your sales process.

If all this sounds confusing, don't worry: it needn't be. AdWords is presented as a great money-grabbing mystery machine by marketing gurus who want you to buy their wares. The essentials, however, are very straightforward and can be tackled one step at a time.

STEP BY STEP Creating a Google AdWords account

As you'll have come to expect, it's entirely free to set up an AdWords account. It's simplest if you already have a Google account (for example on Gmail), so if you don't, I suggest you create one before you begin.

 NEW ACCOUNT First you need to set up your account. Go to http://adwords.google.com and click on Try AdWords Now.

ASSOCIATE YOUR GOOGLE ACCOUNT
On the next screen you're asked whether you have an existing Google account. If not, you'll be taken out of the process to create one. If you do, you can elect to use it or create a new one just for AdWords. I'm not sure what benefit there would be in the latter, unless your main Google account is purely for personal use and you don't want to associate it with AdWords. Click Continue.

GEOGRAPHY LESSON On the next screen you're presented with regional settings. It's absolutely essential you get these right, because Google doesn't allow you to change them later without creating an entirely new account. Click Continue and Google will announce that it's sent a verification email to your email address. Once the verification email arrives, click the link and you'll be taken into AdWords itself for the first time.

TAKE CONTROL Google helpfully presents a button entitled "Create your first campaign", but we're going to ignore this. Why? Well, by following the wizard-based setup procedure and leaving the options set to the default, you would end up with a campaign that devolves more decisions to Google than is ideal. The option is there for people who want to get up and running as quickly as possible, but I don't believe that such a campaign is likely to be effective. You need to take control from the outset and make choices that make sense for you and your campaign, rather than simply leaving Google to spend up to your daily limit.

So I recommend you click the link for creating advanced campaigns under "For experienced advertisers", even though you're only just starting out. Don't worry: the process is very similar to what you would get by clicking the big button at the top, it's just that you're taking more control.

The key, as I've mentioned in our general discussion of pay-per-click campaigns, is to plan carefully and then experiment methodically. You shouldn't expect your AdWords campaign to "just work". Even if it did reap instant results, there would be every chance you could obtain an even better response by tweaking your adverts and keywords. This is something we'll go into in even more depth over the coming pages.

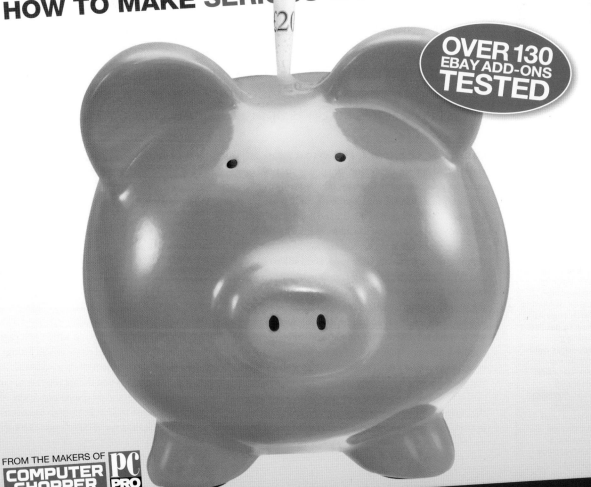

Setting up your AdWords campaign

It's time to roll up your sleeves and get started, beginning with Google AdWords. The "campaign" is AdWords' highest level of organisation. Ad Groups are made up of one or more ads, and campaigns are made up of one or more Ad Groups. Your campaign's settings apply to all Ad Groups and ads within it.

LOCATION, LOCATION, LOCATION Billing, budgets and regional options are among the choices you need to make for your campaign. Unless you have a truly global product, you should set your location according to your audience. If you're based in the UK and selling a physical product, in most cases you'll want to specify the UK as your target location; if you were living in France, but still planning to target mainly UK buyers, you'd still pick UK.

There aren't many situations in which you would leave the location set to Global. This is because your ads and the landing pages they link to must be optimised to appeal to your target audience, and audiences will vary around the world, requiring different techniques and different language – indeed, different languages! – to achieve a reasonable conversion rate. So even if you have a truly global product, you should normally have one campaign per region.

Generally speaking, Google allows you to target at the regional and country level (along with individual states in the US), and you should specify the most focused location you possibly can. If you offer a service in a local area, you can set your campaign to appear in specific cities.

SEARCH OPTIONS At the campaign level, you can also decide in which search engines your ads will appear and on which devices. You have three basic choices: Google Search, Search Partners (including AOL and Virgin Media) and the Content Network. When setting up a new campaign, Google recommends you have your ads shown across "All available sites and devices". This is a bad idea: Google is the only beneficiary. To begin with, you should set every new campaign to Google Search only. This is because each of the three options should be treated differently.

Begin with Google Search and get your campaign operating profitably before adding Search Partners to that campaign. When your campaign is working profitably across Google Search and the Search Partners, you can then set up a separate campaign for the Content Network. The Content

The dashboard for an AdWords campaign. From the graphs, can you guess when I gave Google experimental control of my ad bidding? It was a very short experiment...

Network (where the ads appear within web pages) is a completely different beast to sponsored listings, and needs to be treated with caution.

Google lets you choose whether to target mobile devices as well as standard computers. Again, when setting up it makes sense to limit yourself to computers initially, unless your product specifically targets the mobile market.

AD ROTATION Once you've created an Ad Group, you'll be able to decide how Google rotates your ads, if you have more than one (as you should). Rotation means that instead of showing the same ad every time someone's search matches your keywords, Google will cycle through all those you've created.

By default, Google will give preference to ads with higher click-through rates, so as some of your ads start to outperform others, they'll appear more often. This might seem logical, but it prevents you testing which ads work best. Instead, instruct Google to show your ads in strict rotation, otherwise you'll end up with a lot of detail about one ad and nothing about the others.

The key point is to think carefully about all your choices when setting up a campaign. Aim to focus closely on your target audience while handling each aspect of the campaign yourself. Don't leave it to Google.

STEP BY STEP Enter your campaign settings

1 **FIRST STEPS** If you don't have a Google AdWords account, see p104. Then go to http://adwords.google.com and sign in with your Google account details. Click "Create your first campaign". Bear in mind that Google is presenting the line of least resistance with this process, and many of its settings won't suit you.

2 **DETAILS** On the Campaign Settings screen, give your campaign a name. Under Locations, select the narrowest range of locations that will ensure your most profitable audience sees your ad. For example, GreetingCardMaker.co.uk allows users to create cards and print them on their own printer, so it could be used anywhere in the world, but some users will want the cards printed for them (at a cost) and this would only be possible for users in the UK, at least to begin with. It therefore makes no sense to advertise outside the UK.

Under "Networks, devices and extensions", click "Let me choose" and deselect all options except "Google Search". You should get your campaign running effectively on the main network before adding Search Partners

or Content Network. Unless you're targeting mobile devices specifically, deselect that. All this reduces the number of variables in the campaign, making it easier to tweak.

Under "Bidding and Budget", again reject Google's recommendation. Select "Manual bidding for clicks" so you can specify how much each click is worth to you, rather than having Google modify your bid using its own algorithms (and to suit its own purposes). Ultimately, you want to pay as little as you can to achieve a good position in the sponsored listings: you can only do this by manually setting bid prices and noting where this ranks you. It's an iterative process that can't be bypassed.

You now need to set your budget. The maxim is simple: never set a budget higher than you can afford. Google spreads it over a month, so on any given day your actual costs might exceed the daily limit set here, but not by much. For most new campaigns, I recommend setting the budget between £5 and £10, unless you're sure a higher amount will be profitable or you feel you can afford to risk more. Remember, if for some reason a lot of users suddenly click your ad, your bill can rise precipitously.

Apocryphal tales are told of advertisers losing thousands of pounds over a weekend. Whether you believe them or not, this is the place to prevent it. If in doubt, err on the low side; you can raise it later.

3 **FIRST AD** Click Save and Continue, and Google will ask you to create your first ad. I recommend putting dummy text in here until you set up your Ad Groups (overleaf). Enter your primary keyword in the keyword box. You need to set a cost per click (CPC); to do that, click Estimate Search Traffic and pick a value below the lowest estimate. Again, err on the lower side. Google will now take you through the billing process. My only advice here is to use a credit card to get up and running quickly.

4 **HOLD ON** Once you've finished with billing, Google will automatically turn on your campaign. You don't want that yet, so immediately click the Campaigns tab, click Enabled and select Pause. You now have a campaign that's inactive but ready for you to add keywords and ads.

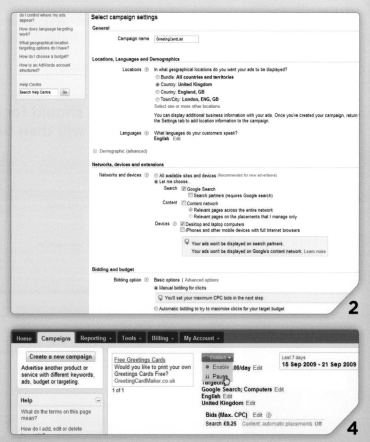

Creating your Ad Groups

The aim of your marketing (and your business) is to make a profit. So you need to attract the maximum profitable traffic to your site for the lowest possible cost. In general, the higher up Google's Sponsored Listings your ad appears, the more clicks you'll get – but, all else being equal, you'll need to bid more for those positions, squeezing your profitability. Fortunes have been lost chasing the top positions purely by bidding more.

The key is to understand how the Google bidding process works. Whenever a search term is typed into Google, it holds an "auction" among the potential advertisers and determines where each ad will appear. Google assigns each ad a "Quality Score" out of ten and then calculates its "Ad Rank" by multiplying the Quality Score by the maximum bid.

For example, let's say there are two advertisers. The first has set a maximum cost per click of £1 and the other 50p. If they both have the same Quality Score (QS), the first advertiser will appear above the second, because they've bid more. However, if the first advertiser has a QS of 2 and an Ad Rank of 2 (£1 × 2) and the second has a QS of 5, then the second will appear above the first, because they have an Ad Rank of 2.5 (£0.50 × 5).

Take a moment to think about that. It's possible to pay half as much as your competition and yet appear above them in the Sponsored Listings. This is why understanding Google's Quality Score is probably the single most important aspect of AdWords: it can singlehandedly turn a struggling campaign into a profitable one.

So how does Google work out the Quality Score of an ad? It looks at three things: the ad's historical click-through rate, the relevance of the ad (there's that word "relevance" again), and the landing page to which it directs the user. But it doesn't give equal weight to each. By far the most important of these three is the click-through rate. Why? Because by using CTR, Google is asking searchers to vote with their clicks to

"Each Ad Group should focus on one of your main keyword groups. The ads will then be more relevant to those keywords."

Very popular, broad keywords such as "holiday" are hugely competitive on Google and will rarely be profitable. Avoid them.

Your **Ad** Here
Use Ad Groups to optimise **your**
pay-per-click advertising
www.sortout**your**adgroups.com

decide whose ad is the most pertinent for their search. CTR accounts for around 60% of the QS, relevance around 30%, and the advertiser's landing page only 10%. (Relevance, in this context, relates to how well the text of your ad correlates with the search term.)

To put it another way, 90% of the Quality Score is determined by the ad itself. The quality of your landing page is important for its own reasons (principally conversion), but as long as the main bases are covered, the focus of your attention when it comes to getting economical traffic should be on the ads themselves.

SETTING UP YOUR AD GROUPS Each Ad Group should focus on one of your main keyword groups. The primary reason for this is that if you create an ad group for each main keyword, the ads will be more relevant to those keywords. For example, if you were an aquarium supplier you might decide that two of your keyword groups would be "cold water fish" and "aquariums". Putting each of these into its own Ad Group means you can write ads aimed specifically at people looking for goldfish, and separate ads for those looking to buy a tank.

The result is a more relevant ad that will have a higher click-through rate. This will mean you need to pay less per click to appear high in the Sponsored Listings. You can also point each ad at a specific landing page, which will increase your conversion rate.

There are four "match" types for keywords. The default is Broad Match: in this case, Google will use fuzzy

logic to match your ad to the keywords typed in. So "card making" would appear for "card making", "making cards" and "making greeting cards", among many others. Phrase Match (denoted by enclosing your keywords in quotes) requires that the searcher type in the exact phrase, so "making cards" wouldn't appear in the above example, but if the user typed "custom card making", then it would.

Exact Match (denoted by enclosing your keywords in square brackets) requires that only the keyword has been typed in, so a search can contain only "card making" and nothing else. Finally, there's the negative match (denoted by a minus sign), where any search containing that word will not display your ad.

As a rule, begin with Broad Match and narrow it down as you find the most profitable keyword combinations.

WRITING YOUR ADS Remember you're trying to achieve two things with your ad copy. First, and most importantly, you need the highest possible CTR of profitable traffic. Don't make the mistake of thinking that maximum traffic is your aim. Visitors who click on your ad but don't buy anything have cost you money; you need to convert enough of them to make a profit.

The second aim is to make sure your ad appears relevant to Google. Both of these reduce your AdWords costs. Including the keywords in the ad body and title will increase relevance. Usually, it will increase CTR as well because Google will show these keywords in bold, making your ad stand out more. ➔

Ad Groups let you build clusters of keywords and test multiple versions of the ad you create for each group, enabling you to carry out a comprehensive analysis of exactly which keywords and messages combine to give you profitable CTR and, ultimately, conversion rates.

1
2

3
4

STEP BY STEP Set up an Ad Group

You've created a campaign with one ad, which is paused (see p107). It's now time to get your ads up and running.

 KEYWORDS Go back to your AdWords campaign and click the Ads tab. You'll find your existing ad there. In the Keywords tab, enter your keywords, one per line. For any negative keywords (see p101), add a minus sign: for example, "-free".

Click the pencil icon to open the inline editor and edit the headline, ad body, display URL and destination URL. The display URL is the web address seen in your ad; the destination URL is the one users are actually taken to if they click. Arguably these ought to be the same, but the display URL can have a significant impact on your click-through rate (CTR) and Google's rules are fairly liberal at present, although you are limited to 35 characters. Your ad will be allowed as long as the display URL points to the same domain as the destination URL. You don't need to include "www", you can use capitalisation to make the text more eye-catching, and you can put almost any text after the domain name.

 SECOND AD After clicking Save, you can make your second ad by selecting Text Ad from the New Ad drop-down menu. (Get your text ads working profitably before you consider the other types.) Create your new ad using the editor. At this stage you should use substantially different text so that you get a clear result when you split-test the two ads. As

time goes on, you will make smaller and smaller changes. You can see in this example that I've changed the headline and body copy of the ad but left the display URL and landing page the same. The target audience of both ads is exactly the same, but we're looking at which form of wording gets the most profitable traffic.

 OTHER VARIABLES In this example I've made four ads. There are only two variations of the ads themselves: the difference is that one points to my site's home page and the other to a custom-made landing page. So we're testing two things at once: the performance of the ads and (once we've set up conversion tracking) the effectiveness of the landing page.

 ROTATION Finally, go to Campaign Settings > Advanced Settings. Click Ad delivery, Ad rotation, Frequency capping, and pick "Rotate: Show ads more evenly". You'll be warned that most advertisers leave this set to Optimise. That's because most campaigns aren't actively managed in the way yours will be. If you intend to set the ads up and leave Google to manage them, by all means pick Optimise, but actively managing campaigns is the only way to make them pay in a competitive market. By choosing to have your ads shown evenly, you're ensuring all variations get enough clicks to enable you to choose a winner quickly. You can then delete the losing ad and create yet another variation of the winning ad to test.

→ If there is a true AdWords guru, it's Perry Marshall (www.perrymarshall.com). In his *Definitive Guide to AdWords 2010*, he identifies four stages to go through to create the best-performing ad:

1 Message
2 Word ordering
3 Words
4 Punctuation

MESSAGE Your ad should reflect whatever is unique about your business and what it offers. Do you supply something free that others charge for? Does your product or service give better results than others? Do you have a guarantee? (And if not, why not?) What is the specific deal you're offering?

Take a look at this ad for PassYourTheory.co.uk, which appeared when users did a Google search on the keywords "hazard perception":

> ## Hazard Perception 2009/10
> Join & PASS. New Official Questions
> DSA Hazard Video. Pass Guarantee!
> PassYourTheory.co.uk/Hazard-Test

This features three of our service's most important features: first, that we are official licensees of the DSA; second, that we have the very latest questions; and finally, that we offer a pass guarantee. How do we know that our potential members are interested in these things? Because we have asked them in a survey and we have tested which features result in the best conversion rate.

Here's an Amazon ad (below) in similar vein. It was triggered by the search phrase "buy Sony A200K". Notice how it's very specific about the free delivery offer (an Amazon feature) and the price. Given the word "buy", Amazon is gambling on being cheaper than the other advertisers, so it shows its price in the headline. As it happens, this ad commits the cardinal sin of leading to a page that doesn't offer what the ad promises: the camera is available (it's an old model) but not for the stated price! Be warned: Amazon may be able to get away with this, but mere mortals cannot.

> ## Sony DSLR-A200K - £305
> Digital SLR Camera + Lens18-70mm
> Buy Now. Free Delivery.
> www.amazon.co.uk/Sony

WORD ORDERING You should start by running ads that feature various iterations of your product's main features, and test them until you find out which ones trigger the best conversion rate. Once you've done this, you can alter the specific wording. A classic technique is to swap the second and third lines around; you'd be surprised at the difference this can make.

WORDS You should also test the effect of swapping specific words. In general, you should only test one word-swap at a time – otherwise the results will be impossible to analyse – so this stage should be carried out after the other two described above. Getting your message right is likely to yield bigger improvements in CTR and conversion than changes to word order or word selection. Make sure you get your keywords into the message: if at all possible they should appear in the title, in one of the body lines, and in the display URL.

PUNCTUATION Finally, test the effect of adding commas, exclamation marks (Google only allows one per ad) and dashes. Capitalising The First Letter Of Every Word can also be effective in grabbing attention and provoking more clicks – but it must be tested.

There are dozens of tips and tricks you can use to improve your CTR and conversion, but the key is to remember to communicate your main messages – and only promise what you can actually deliver.

CREATING AD GROUPS Google is quite happy if you create only one ad in an Ad Group, but you should always have at least two, and usually more. This is because you need to test both the effectiveness of the ads themselves and the process the visitor goes through after arriving at your site. Clicking on the ad is just the first step; Google lets you track visitors right through the process, whether you want them to buy from you or sign up to a mailing list.

This process has two steps: creating your landing page – the page on your site at which visitors arrive when they click the ad – and setting up conversion tracking. If you're going to use a landing page other than your main home page, it might be worth creating this now (see overleaf). Alternatively, if you'd prefer to take your time over this, you could get the Ad Group up and running first.

On the opposite page, I'll take you through the vital first steps. You may be tempted to launch your campaign as soon as you finish this and use your home page as your initial landing page. All you'd then need to do is set up conversion tracking. However, if you're serious about your AdWords campaign you should really create a custom landing page from the beginning. My experience is that they're always more effective than your home page.

Good-quality classified ads are an excellent source of inspiration for your online ad copy, since they do the same basic job of getting response from readers.

Designing a landing page

The landing page is the main entry point to your website and probably the most important page on the site. Over the next four pages, I'm going to concentrate on how to get it right. The first thing to understand is that landing pages have two purposes. The first and most important reason is to convert more visitors into buyers. However, in doing this you need to take care not to damage your AdWords campaign.

Remember, Google takes your landing page into account when it works out your Quality Score, and this heavily influences how much your ads will cost. While it's true that the landing page is the least important of the three factors (the others being click-through rate and relevance, as we saw on p108), it represents around 10% of your Quality Score, so it could make the difference between appearing in position 4 or 5 in the Sponsored Listings.

The good news is that Google looks for exactly the same features in your page as your visitors will, so by optimising the page to suit potential customers, you're also optimising it for Google. In the bad old days, landing pages were known as "squeeze pages", and the prevailing wisdom was that they should have no links to the rest of your site and no distractions: their one purpose was to get a visitor to give up their email address. However, both your visitors and Google will respond poorly to such tactics. Visitors will leave in droves, and Google will lower your Quality Score.

ANATOMY OF A LANDING PAGE Generally speaking, each Ad Group in your campaign should lead to its own unique landing page. To be effective, a landing page must closely match the ads that lead to it. Contrast this with your site's home page. Until a few years ago, the home page was considered to be the most common entry point, since most visitors arrived by typing the URL directly into their browser or via an old-style "directory" search engine. Nowadays, search engines index individual pages rather than entire sites, so home pages have become much less important and should not be the destination for your ads.

If a visitor types "natural back pain relief" into their browser and sees an ad saying, effectively, "we sell natural back-pain relief, buy it here", then they expect, when they click the ad, to see a page selling that back-pain remedy – not the front page of a site that might be selling remedies for dozens of different ailments. You need to make the buying process as simple, short and obvious as possible.

Jay Abraham's 100 Best Headlines (www.pcpro.co.uk/links/headlines) is an excellent source of inspiration for your landing page writing.

There's a well-established typical structure for a landing page, which you can quickly reproduce using my template. The key elements – headline, navigation, copy and call to action – are explained below.

Each landing page is made up of two parts: a series of benefits, whose aim is to allow the customer to evaluate whether your product meets their needs, and, crucially, a very clear call to action. In other words, you need to make it abundantly obvious what action you want the user to take, whether that's to buy now or sign up to a mailing list. The main elements of your page should be:

1 Headline
2 Navigation
3 Copy
4 Call to action

THE HEADLINE It's essential your headline closely reflects the ad. It should include your keywords and make the immediate point that the visitor has arrived in the right place. For 100 excellent headline examples, go to www.pcpro.co.uk/links/headlines – but the main thing to remember is that the headline must encourage the visitor to stay for long enough to read the copy.

Your headline should be short, relevant and inviting. If you can make it witty as well, so much the better, but the most important factor is relevance. Using the back pain example, the headline should refer directly to

the solution you offer to back pain: if it doesn't, the visitor, having clicked your ad under the impression that it would lead to back-pain remedies, is likely to click the Back button immediately, and your advertising is wasted.

NAVIGATION Traditional "squeeze pages" had no navigation, and when it became obvious that Google punishes such pages with low-quality scores (because of the lack of links), marketers simply added navigation at the bottom of the page. The thinking behind this is that you don't want people to wander off around your site when you're trying to get them to carry out a particular action. Whether there is any merit in this theory is debatable, and it will vary from site to site, but the fact is that you can't get away without putting navigation in. Specifically, you should include not only links to other parts of your site, but also to your privacy policy and contact details. Users expect it, and if they want a link but can't find one, they'll just click Back.

My belief is that navigation, if it's going to be there, should be at the top of the page, where it's most useful to your visitors, either just above the headline or just below it. As with so many other aspects of your marketing, however, you should test the position (on multiple landing pages) to see if it affects your profitability. ➜

"A few years ago, the home page was the most common entry point to a website. Nowadays, search engines lead users to individual pages, so home pages have become much less important and should not be the destination for your ads."

3 | Marketing
Find new customers

→ **COPY** Internet marketers continue to debate whether "long" or "short" copy is more effective. Again, the only way to be sure is to test it, but my experience has been that long copy tends to outperform short. Why? Probably because people who prefer short copy can always skim through the longer form, whereas those who want to read more before making a decision won't find what they need in a short version.

Landing-page copy tends to be conversational in style, and the best landing pages include elements of storytelling in their construction. This, if done well, has the effect of drawing the reader into the copy and giving a structure within which to outline your benefits.

Having said that long copy tends to be more effective, that doesn't mean the text should be dense. Inserting bullet points and numbered lists, along with graphics and photos, will help to break up the text and keep the reader interested. It also makes it easier for visitors who prefer short copy to skip their way through the page, picking up the important messages.

THE POWER OF YOU It's essential to write copy from the point of view of your audience. The market research you did when planning your business pays off here: you should know who your customers are and how they talk. I'm not suggesting you mimic their language – people don't necessarily buy from someone who communicates as they do – but you can at least avoid putting them off. For example, if you're selling to teenagers (good luck with that!) then writing your copy in "text-speak" is unlikely to work, but it would make sense to visit sites that are popular with that group and emulate their writing style.

The word "you" should appear throughout, and the features of your product should be expressed as benefits for your target audience. For example, a candle-making kit might include high-quality metal moulds, but what does this mean for the buyer? The benefit of the metal mould is that it can be re-used many times, reducing the ongoing cost of candle making – so say so.

A final note on testimonials. Testimonials (recommendations of your product and/or company from real customers) are unquestionably important to have on your site, and it might seem obvious that you should include them in landing pages. But I have now tested this twice and, for my sites at least, testimonials have actually reduced the conversion rate. It doesn't make sense (which is one of the reasons I've tested it twice), but the page containing testimonials reduced conversions by almost a quarter. My recommendation is to include a few and test against a page without them.

STEP BY STEP
Build a landing page that works

There's a definite generic "look and feel" to the standard landing page. The design tends to be minimal, with a central white rectangle containing the copy, links and pictures. This rectangle is centred horizontally, and narrow enough to fit a reasonable minimum monitor resolution. The only problem, if you've created your site using WordPress, is that it's difficult to have WordPress apply one design to the site as a whole and a different one to the landing page.

Fortunately, this straightforward design makes it quite simple to create your landing page in HTML and CSS. Of course, you can still add links between this page and your WordPress site. Once you've established a look and feel, the same code can be re-used as the basis for all your landing pages. To get started, you can download my landing page template from www.scribbleit.co.uk/landingpages/template.zip.

1 **ADAPT THE TEMPLATE** Unzip the template and you'll find that there are two folders: images and css. Double-click landingpage1.html to view the template. You'll see there are a number of placeholder sections and graphics for you to replace. This should give you the opportunity to concentrate most of your efforts on getting the copy right.

2 **CHANGE THE CSS** Open the file landingpage.css and you'll see it's a bog standard fixed-width centred layout. If you want to change the body copy font, find the "body" type selector. Within that, you can alter the "font-family" attribute, sticking to the range of "web safe" fonts found on most computers (see p54). You can also change the background colour within the body selector – this manifests itself as the colour of the surround – along with the default text colour (using the "color" property).

The heading fonts can be altered in the <h1> and <h2> selectors. If you want to change the width of the main frame, find the outer "wrapper id" selector and change the width value there. It's currently set to

800px, which is ultra-safe: it wouldn't be too risky to increase this to 1,000px if you want extra space, although this may be too wide for netbooks, for example.

You'll find a file called logo.jpg in the /images folder: replace it with your own logo or banner. I've also included placeholders for two pictures, both floated to the right-hand side. If you want photos, diagrams or graphics, just replace these placeholders with your artwork and amend the <img> tags within landingpage1.html. It's good practice to include one or more pictures in your initial design and then test whether they are effective.

3 **WRITE THE COPY** Having got the landing page looking right, spend the majority of your time writing compelling copy that sells the benefits of

your product or service. Go through the text in the template and replace it with your own. If you have genuine customer testimonials, I suggest including a limited number at this point and testing their effectiveness. Keep in mind that your purpose is to get your visitor to take a specific action: make sure there's no doubt exactly what this is. Get someone else to read the copy to make sure. You'd be amazed how many landing pages leave potential customers wondering what to do.

4 **UPLOAD THE FILES** Once your HTML and CSS files are complete, use FileZilla to copy the landing page and its folders to your web space. I suggest creating a folder for your landing pages to ensure they remain separate from the files for your WordPress site.

Running your AdWords campaign

Once your campaign is up and running, there are plenty of numbers to keep track of. Some of these are instantly available within your AdWords dashboard, but others aren't. Take it from me: you should never run an AdWords campaign without setting up conversion tracking. It's the road to business failure.

The seven key metrics for an AdWords campaign are impressions, clicks, click-through rate (CTR), cost per click, conversion number, conversion rate and cost per conversion. The first four are always shown in the AdWords control panel, requiring no further work to set up, but the conversion rate and cost-per-conversion figures aren't, and they're by far the most important. Running a campaign without checking the conversion figures means you have no way of knowing how much you're spending in marketing per sale; and without this, you can't tell if your campaign is profitable. So it's essential to track conversions, and I'll show you (on p118) how to set up the code for this.

Here's what to look for in each of the three main categories of data.

IMPRESSIONS Every time an ad is seen, that's an "impression". In the Keywords tab, you can see how many of those impressions were triggered by each keyword. If you order the list by impressions, you'll see which keywords generated the most views of your ad. This is the first time

Impressions

		Ad group	Status ?	Search Max. CPC	Content Auto Max. CPC ?	Clicks	Impr.	CTR ?	Avg. CPC ?	Cost	Avg. Pos.	Conv. (1-per-click) ?	Cost / conv. (1-per-click) ?	Conv. rate (1-per-click) ?
☐	●	life in the uk	Eligible	£0.05	auto	88	3,720	2.37%	£0.04	£3.93	4.2	12	£0.33	13.64%
☐	●	citizenship	Eligible	£0.05	auto	55	1,428	3.85%	£0.04	£2.47	3.8	8	£0.31	14.55%
☐	●	British Citizenship	Eligible	£0.05	auto	47	4,995	0.94%	£0.05	£2.14	9.3	9	£0.24	19.15%
						179	6,013	2.98%	£0.05	£8.11	4	27	£0.30	15.08%

Clicks

		Ad group	Status ?	Search Max. CPC	Content Auto Max. CPC ?	Clicks	Impr.	CTR ?	Avg. CPC ?	Cost	Avg. Pos.	Conv. (1-per-click) ?	Cost / conv. (1-per-click) ?	Conv. rate (1-per-click) ?
☐	●	life in the uk	Eligible	£0.05	auto	88	3,720	2.37%	£0.04	£3.93	4.2	12	£0.33	13.64%
☐	●	citizenship	Eligible	£0.05	auto	55	1,428	3.85%	£0.04	£2.47	3.8	8	£0.31	14.55%
☐	●	British Citizenship	Eligible	£0.05	auto	47	4,995	0.94%	£0.05	£2.14	9.3	9	£0.24	19.15%
						179	6,013	2.98%	£0.05	£8.11	4	27	£0.30	15.08%

Conversions

		Ad group	Status ?	Search Max. CPC	Content Auto Max. CPC ?	Clicks	Impr.	CTR ?	Avg. CPC ?	Cost	Avg. Pos.	Conv. (1-per-click) ?	Cost / conv. (1-per-click) ?	Conv. rate (1-per-click) ?
☐	●	life in the uk	Eligible	£0.05	auto	88	3,720	2.37%	£0.04	£3.93	4.2	12	£0.33	13.64%
☐	●	citizenship	Eligible	£0.05	auto	55	1,428	3.85%	£0.04	£2.47	3.8	8	£0.31	14.55%
☐	●	British Citizenship	Eligible	£0.05	auto	47	4,995	0.94%	£0.05	£2.14	9.3	9	£0.24	19.15%
						179	6,013	2.98%	£0.05	£8.11	4	27	£0.30	15.08%

you'll have real statistics (as opposed to estimates) from Google about the popularity of your keywords.

CLICKS "Clicks" is the number of times the ad was actually clicked. Again, you can see the number of clicks for each keyword under the Keywords tab. Your click-through rate (CTR) is the percentage of impressions that result in a click.

Too many AdWords advertisers concentrate on these three figures, especially the click-through rate. By working on impressions and CTR you can maximise traffic, but remember, you're charged per click. If you drive up your CTR but the percentage of people who buy from you goes down, you can turn a profitable business into a disaster. The classic example is when you put words such as "free" in your ad: this will drive lots of traffic, but the people arriving at your site are unlikely to be in the mood to pay for anything.

CONVERSIONS A "conversion" is when a visitor takes an action you want them to take. This is usually signing up to an email list (which you hope will result in a purchase later) or making an immediate purchase. In many cases, there are numerous steps between the initial search and the purchase, so – unlike the other figures – the conversion rate is affected by much more than just the quality and position of your ad.

However, the number of conversions, the conversion rate and the cost per conversion are by far the most important three figures you can track, and Google's "roundtrip" tracking allows you to see the exact marketing cost per sale. To put it simply, if you sell a product for £10 and your cost per conversion is £20, you're in trouble. If the figures were reversed but you only made two conversions a week, you'd also have a problem. In an ideal world, you're looking for a high number of conversions, a good conversion rate and a profitable cost per conversion.

GOOD NUMBERS Newcomers to internet marketing often ask what click-through rate and conversion rate they should be aiming at. This will vary from market to market and business to business, but you should always be aiming to maximise these figures (except where increasing the CTR reduces the conversion rate) so that you make a profit.

To give some rules of thumb, successful internet businesses tend to have a conversion rate in the range of 0.75% to 2%. Some may be much higher, but very few profitable business are lower. A conversion rate of, say, 0.5% requires 200 visitors per sale; if that traffic has been paid for via AdWords, then clearly the product would have to have a high purchase price to be profitable.

THE GOLDEN TWO Broadly speaking, when it comes to judging whether one ad is performing better than another, you should be concentrating on clicks and click-through ➜

What really matters is how many people buy from you and how much profit you make on each sale, taking into account the cost of your marketing. The calculations could get complicated, but if you set it up correctly, Google will do the numbers for you.

➜ rate. At the same time, you must check that any increase in these figures isn't cancelled out by a drop in conversions.

Overall, the two most critical figures to keep your eye on are the number of conversions and the cost per conversion. These sum up the profitability, or otherwise, of your business, since one is an indicator of your turnover and the other of what is likely to be your main cost of doing business. If you spot that the number of conversions drops or the cost per conversion rises, take immediate action to work out why this might be and what to do about it. More often than not, you'll find something's changed in your marketplace or in the shopping cart process that acts as a barrier to conversions. For example, a competitor might have entered the market or may be running a promotion.

CONVERSION TRACKING Since the conversion figures are so important, you need to set up conversion tracking through AdWords. It's free and pretty easy to do, and it's the single factor that separates the serious, profitable, businessperson from the half-hearted dabbler. After all, if you don't know how much each conversion costs, you're missing out on the most important piece of financial data. You're running an AdWords campaign blind.

Google begins tracking when the user clicks the ad, and registers a conversion when they complete whatever action you specify, whether that's a purchase, a sign-up, or even that the user visits a particular page. Conversion tracking works by saving a cookie to the visitor's computer when they click on your ad. This cookie has a life of 30 days, and any conversion that takes place within that period is recorded. Google will also track multiple conversions – for example, if the user comes back and buys again – and can report this in your AdWords interface.

The conversion statistics are displayed alongside each of your ad variations, so you can see immediately which ads result in the highest number of conversions at the lowest cost. Believe me, once you start seeing the figures, they'll exert an irresistible pull on you – which is a good thing! They also build up a long-term record of your business's performance.

DON'T LEAP TOO EARLY One final word of warning: don't pay any attention to your figures until you have enough to be statistically valid. In most cases, you should have at least 25 conversions before taking any action. At a conversion rate of 1%, this means you'd need 2,500 clicks and, at a typical CTR of 5%, around 50,000 impressions. Patience is needed. Once you do have enough data, however, don't delay acting on it: in the beginning you will usually see a definitive winner when comparing ads, so the first step is to pause or delete the losing ad and make a new copy of the winning one to alter and test again.

How to track conversions in Google AdWords

The only way to know if your marketing is profitable is to set up conversion tracking. It's a reasonably straightforward task, but you need to get it right.

1 NAME YOUR ACTION From your AdWords Control Panel, select Conversion Tracking and then click the New Action link on the Conversion Tracking summary page. On the "Create an Action" page, give your action a name to help identify it – you can track multiple conversion types, so it's important to differentiate between them – and then choose the most appropriate action type from the drop-down list. If each customer is worth a fixed amount in your business model, you can specify that in the "Revenue for your action" box. In most cases, though, this will be left blank.

The rest of the page can be left as it is. Note that Google insists you notify your customers that you're adding a cookie; this can have security implications, but these days the vast majority of users are happy to accept them. The easiest way to add the notification is to use one of the pre-existing text formats offered here. If you choose None, Google will check to see if you notify the customer independently; you can't get away without mentioning it to users at all.

2 GET THE CODE Once you're done, click Save Action & Get Code. This provides you with the JavaScript code to insert in the page of your site on which the action occurs. If it's an email list sign-up, for example, it'll be the confirmation screen that the user reaches when they've completed the sign-up process. If it's a purchase, you would insert the code on the order confirmation screen. Make it something that the user must see if they actually complete the action, but will never see if they don't. In any case, select the code here and copy it to the clipboard by pressing <Ctrl-C>.

3 INSERT THE CODE If you're using WordPress, the simplest approach is to install the Google Website Optimizer for WordPress plugin. Although we aren't actually using the Website Optimizer, the plugin is fine for hosting your conversion tracking code. With that installed in the usual way (see p79), go to the page containing whatever you've decided to track and tick "Enable the

1

2

3

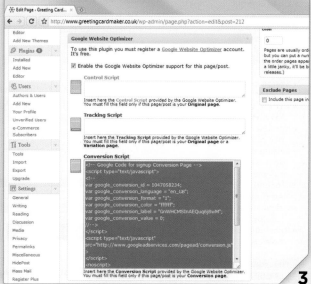

4

Google Website Optimizer support for this page/post". Paste the JavaScript code into the Conversion Script field, leaving the other two blank. Save the page.

 AND NOW WAIT... That's all there is to it. Unfortunately, conversion tracking doesn't perform any immediate checks to see if the code is in the right place, so you'll need to wait a day or two to make sure you have some data coming through. How long this takes will depend on how busy your site is. To check your figures, click the Ads tab

in your Campaign Management panel on the Google AdWords site and you should see figures appearing in the Conv, Cost/Conv and Conv.rate columns (assuming you've sold anything, of course).

Don't jump to any conclusions until you have enough conversions to make a judgement. The more ads you have, the longer this will take. In this example, the cost per conversion of one of the ads is three times more than one of the others. That may seem like a conclusive result, but there simply haven't been enough conversions yet to be sure.

The importance of split testing

Today's internet business technologies offer previously unimaginable ways to test your marketing. The simplest, and one of the most effective, is A/B split testing. You try one approach on half your audience and another on the other half, and see what happens. The results can be very surprising.

A typical use of this kind of testing is when you want to optimise your landing pages – the pages where visitors arrive after clicking your ads. Instead of bringing every user who clicks a particular ad to the same web page, you send them at random to one of two different pages. Then you wait and see which route gets you the most conversions. It's just one of a seemingly infinite number of methods to refine your marketing. You don't have to rely on "gut instinct" or accepted wisdom to dictate the way you sell: you can try alternative ideas and see within a few weeks exactly how they perform.

Landing-page split testing can be set up using the Website Optimizer, part of the Google AdWords toolset. The process is slightly more involved than setting up conversion tracking, but it's easy enough if you follow the steps closely, and won't interfere with your conversion tracking code.

1 **START THE EXPERIMENT** Begin by selecting Website Optimizer, which you'll find under either Tools or Reporting. You may be prompted to create a Google Analytics account if you don't already have one (see p92).

Click the "Create another experiment" link and select A/B Experiment from the options presented. (The other option, Multivariate, should only be attempted once you've broadly optimised your landing page and you're getting lots of traffic to provide statistically meaningful data.) The next page presents the series of steps you must already have completed. Click the checkbox and select the Create button. On the setup page, give your experiment an appropriate name and then tell Google which two pages to test. In this case I'm testing the home page of PassYourCitizenship against my first try at a landing page.

On my PassYourCitizenship website, the landing page (left) hugely outperformed the home page (right) when tested with Google's tools.

Finally, tell Google which page the user has to reach to qualify as a conversion. Here I'm testing which of the two is more effective at getting the user to the sign-up page. Once I've got the landing page broadly working, I'll change the conversion page to my PayPal confirmation page, so I'm only including paid members in my figures. I won't do that immediately because fewer visitors will reach that point, so it would take much longer to get useful results.

On the next page, select "You will install and validate the JavaScript tags" and click Continue.

2 **ADD THE CODE** Google now presents the code that needs to be copied into the various pages of your site. The first two blocks are for the top and bottom of your "original" page (the home page in this case, as opposed to the variation you're testing). The first block controls whether the user sees the original or the variation. It makes the choice randomly, but will present the same page to the same visitor if they come back later.

If you're not using a content management system, you'll have to copy and paste this code manually into your pages. If you're using WordPress, install the Google Website Optimizer for WordPress plugin (which you already have if you followed our guide to conversion tracking on p118).

3 **VALIDATE** The "variation" page (the landing page in this case) needs only one block of JavaScript: paste this immediately before the closing <body> tag. If you're using the WordPress plugin, just go to your landing page via the WordPress Dashboard and paste the code into the appropriate box.

Finally, you need to add the conversion page tracking script to your sign-up or "thank you" page (or whichever page represents a conversion). Once this is done, click Validate Pages and Google will check to see if the code has been installed and is working.

You should now preview your experiment to check that the correct pages are showing up. It's very difficult to change experiments once they're running, so make doubly sure before clicking Start Experiment.

4 **MEASURE OF SUCCESS** You now need to give Google time to collect and process the results. Leave it a day or two, then go back to the Website Optimizer and you'll see your experiment listed. Click View Report to see how it's doing. In all likelihood, it will tell you that it hasn't yet collected enough data to reach a conclusion, so it's a case of checking back to see at which point Google declares a winner: it usually needs at least 100 conversions. In this example, my landing page has outperformed the home page by over 40%. Imagine what a 40% improvement could do for your business!

Home truths

The first split test you should do is create your first landing page and test it against your site's home page. A landing page should almost always be more effective than the home page, so if it isn't, you need to work on the landing page until it is. As an example, I set up an experiment recently where the home page surprisingly performed much better than the landing page – only to find that I'd miscoded the "Sign me up" button on the landing page. With that fixed, the home page was quickly trounced.

1

2

3

4

Watching them watching you

Uninformed preconceptions are the enemy of effective marketing. Never assume anything about how your customers will react to your website or your product. Over the years I have been surprised (and sometimes shocked) so many times that I now take nothing for granted – and nor should you.

As we've seen, you can split-test your AdWords ads to see which are the most effective and use Google's Website Optimizer to test landing-page variations on your website. But what you're doing there is comparing one version against another and selecting whichever is better. This results in step-by-step improvements, but if you want to radically change your understanding of how your site is used by your customers, you need something more.

What if you could see which parts of a page visitors spend longest looking at? Where they scroll to? Or which links on the page they click most often? Until recently this involved running "usability lab" experiments where you watched (or videoed) a limited number of typical visitors interacting with your site, but this is expensive and tends to be a one-off rather than ongoing.

Clicktale (www.clicktale.com) is a JavaScript-powered technology that records the mouse movements of your visitors. By doing this, it can tell how long users spend on specific parts of the page, where they scroll to and what they click on. The results of this tracking can be displayed in "heat map" form: the redder the colour, the more time was spent on that part of the page.

If you know which parts of your landing pages visitors spend more time on, for example, you can ensure your most important messages appear there. You can also see which of your "calls to action" are working: which "sign-up" buttons attract the most attention, whether users prefer links or buttons, which colours work best... You're certain to learn something that will improve effectiveness.

You can also spot logjams and misunderstandings. For example, you might notice visitors clicking on a graphic that you intended just as an illustration. That means they're interested in learning more about whatever it represents. It's as if someone is asking you to tell them more, and by taking them up on it (in this case by linking the graphic to another page) you will connect with your visitors better, build trust and interest, and convert more to sales.

Clicktale offers a free version of its service, and setting it up is a matter of copying two small JavaScript code snippets to the top and bottom of each of the pages you want to track. A few days later, you can view your heat maps, click maps and even Flash movies that show how an individual user has interacted with your page. You won't look at your visitors in the same way again.

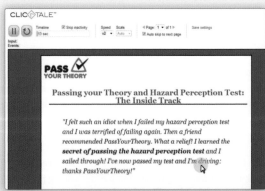

Clicktale's heat map shows which parts of your pages generate the most interest, while movies look over the shoulder of individual users.

Hiya,

Thanks for your ace program, I signed up Monday night for the 3 days and took my test today (Thursday) and passed! Woo hoo! Last time I took the test I failed miserably and thought I would this time too, but after doing the questions time and again and practising on your clips I passed with flying colours, well worth £3.50!!!

Thanks again, Julia

What do they think of you?

Lack of trust is one of the main reasons potential customers don't become buyers. Credit-card fraud, email spam and spyware all work to reduce trust in internet-based businesses. For some customers, if something goes wrong their first instinct is to assume the service they're using is attempting to rip them off. Others won't even consider buying online. So what can you do to increase trust in you and break down those barriers?

SECURITY People do worry about credit-card fraud when they buy online, so reassure them. Your best protection comes from the services you outsource to. If you use PayPal, Nochex or WorldPay, for example, your users' credit-card details are never stored on your server but only on the super-secure servers of those service providers, each of whom has policies to protect customers from fraud.

You will store the email addresses of users who sign up, but by using licensed, reputable autoresponder services and obeying the anti-spam regulations you will ensure that the customer's details remain on your system rather than being stolen by shysters.

All this protection for your customers is of little use from a marketing point of view unless you tell them about it. The simplest way is to include the company logos on your site and, most importantly, on your landing pages. Link the logos to the service providers' consumer protection policy pages (but make sure the link opens a new window or tab rather than overwriting your page – see p91) and, if you meet its requirements, consider joining the SafeBuy (www.safebuy.org.uk) accreditation scheme to further reassure potential buyers.

Incidentally, you must also notify the Information Commissioner's Office that you will be storing personal data, at a cost of £35: see www.ico.gov.uk/what_we_cover/data_protection/notification.aspx.

TESTIMONIALS Nothing builds trust like personal recommendation. Most successful businesses actively encourage word-of-mouth marketing, both by asking their customers to recommend them to friends and family and by asking them directly for testimonials. However cynical you might imagine visitors to be, genuine testimonials can be highly effective. Don't make them up: users will see through it, and this destroys your credibility (as well as constituting false advertising).

The simplest way to get testimonials is to ask customers what they think of you as part of a satisfaction survey. Ask what aspects of your service they value most (and least) and request basic demographic information such as gender and age. This in itself can be priceless: when we first surveyed customers of PassYourTheory.co.uk, we found the people who actually bought from us were not the ones we'd been aiming at. As you can imagine, this radically altered the service and the way we subsequently presented it.

Include in your survey a question asking the customer to summarise what they think of your service, making it clear that you may use their comments on your website while reassuring them that their full name will not appear. The effect of this is that people often write their comments with the intention of them appearing on the website. Clearly, you shouldn't include negative comments, and you should edit any testimonials that are very poorly written – but take care not to change them too much, beyond correcting spelling mistakes: after all, these testimonials are written in the language of your customers.

While I've found that testimonials have a variable effect on my landing pages, other testing has proved beyond any doubt that a dedicated testimonials page significantly increases trust and, therefore, conversion. Potential customers like to know that other people have chosen your product or service and were happy with it. Never underestimate the power of the herd mentality.

Make your business thrive

Once you switch on your pay-per-click advertising campaign, you are immediately visible to your customers and, if you've judged your market properly, the orders will begin arriving. Congratulations: your business is alive, and the initial job of getting up and running is done. From here on, there are many factors that will contribute to your success – luck not the least of them – but following some golden rules will help ensure it.

The three rules we've covered in this book are:

 1 **You must choose or develop the right product**

 2 **You must build an effective platform to sell it**

 3 **You must find and connect with enough of the right customers**

For any individual product or service, steps 1 and 2 take place only once. You'll come back and tweak the product specification or the website, but, assuming you've followed an effective process, your product and site will remain essentially as they are for some time.

Step 3, however, is a never-ending, iterative process. The concept of "build it and they will come" has no place in modern business, if indeed it ever did. If you don't market your product or service effectively, it might as well not exist: no-one will ever know about it, much less buy it.

Having said that, if you've followed this book through, the bulk of the grunt work is behind you. Your AdWords campaign is set up, conversion tracking is installed and you're split-testing your landing pages. All you need

An easy-to-use accounting service such as FreeAgent helps you manage your finances without getting bogged down (see p126).

to do is build time into your day to check your AdWords control panel to see if enough data has been gathered to enable you to make a decision. If it has, don't delay: delete the underperforming ad or landing page, make a copy of the winner, change it and split-test it against the original.

As time goes on, the results of this process will become less and less clear-cut. You may hit the "AdWords ceiling", which is where your changes begin to perform consistently worse than the existing ad or landing page. If you get there, congratulations: you can consider that aspect of your marketing to be optimised, for now at least.

However, there are more tools available to help you drive your business on to even greater success.

 THE ONE REPORT Google AdWords offers a sometimes bewildering array of reports, but the most useful is the Search Query Performance Report (right). This tells you what searches your visitors typed in to find you. You can use this to find new keywords, along with a very good idea of how profitable they're likely to be, as you can see the conversion rate and cost per conversion.

Begin by clicking the Reporting tab in your control panel. Select New Report and, on the Create Report page, select Search Query Performance. The Level of Detail should usually be set to Ad Group and the View to Summary. Set a reasonable date range, depending on traffic but no more than a month. Under Campaigns and Ad Groups, select "Manually select from a list" and click the Add link next to the Ad Group you want to look at. Under Advanced Settings you can add or remove any columns you don't want to include. The most important figures to include are impressions, CTR and conversion stats.

Give the report a name and opt to "Save this as a new report template" to avoid the rigmarole of going through this process again. Optionally, you can have the report run automatically and the results sent to you by

Search Query Report

Report Generated: 13 Oct 2009 17:20:54 Show report detail

Export Report   Create Another Report Like This

6 Oct 2009 - 12 Oct 2009

View: Summary

Impressions	Clicks	CTR	Avg CPC	Cost	Avg Position	Conversions (1-per-click)	Conv. Rate (1-per-click)	Cost/Conv. (1-per-click)
10,252	641	6.25%	£0.05	£33.50	3.48	427	60.40%	£0.09

Campaign	Ad Group	Search Query	Search Query Match Type	Ad Group Status	Campaign Status	Impressions	Clicks	CTR	Avg CPC	Cost	Avg Position	Conversions (1-per-click)	Conv. Rate (1-per-click)	Cost/Conv. (1-per-click)
PassYourCitizenship	life in the uk	life in the uk test	Phrase	Active	Active	6,837	109	1.81%	£0.04	£4.28	4.0	77	65.25%	£0.06
PassYourCitizenship	life in the uk	life in the uk	Exact	Active	Active	1,002	37	3.69%	£0.05	£1.71	2.7	27	62.79%	£0.07
PassYourCitizenship	British Citizenship	british citizenship	Exact	Active	Active	852	39	4.58%	£0.08	£3.06	2.8	26	61.90%	£0.13
PassYourCitizenship	citizenship	citizenship test	Exact	Active	Active	501	77	15.37%	£0.05	£3.52	1.9	54	63.63%	£0.07
PassYourCitizenship	British Citizenship	british citizenship test	Exact	Active	Active	455	83	18.24%	£0.07	£6.17	2.1	60	68.97%	£0.11
PassYourCitizenship	life in the uk	life in the uk test 2009	Phrase	Active	Active	190	8	4.21%	£0.05	£0.40	1.9	9	75.00%	£0.07

Google's Search Query Report (above and left) shows you which words users typed into the search engine when they hit your site.

of line 1. Yet it has a higher click-through rate and an almost identical conversion rate. The reason is immediately obvious: the cost per click (CPC) for line 3 is twice that of line 1.

I can see that ads triggered by "british citizenship" are appearing in a higher average position than "life in the uk test", and this is likely to be the reason for the higher CPC. My first step should be to reduce the bid price for that keyword phrase, and in that way push it down the list a bit.

If you see keywords that have reasonable traffic, high click-through rate and low to moderate cost per conversion, consider splitting them off into separate ad groups. You can then target a specific ad and landing page at them and thus drive down the conversion cost.

KEEP YOUR EYE ON THE DATA Don't feel overwhelmed by the amount of data available. Keep a regular eye on the key figures outlined in "Running an AdWords Campaign" (p116). You can do this directly within the AdWords control panel or by generating an Ad Performance report. This needn't be onerous.

When you first start up a campaign, you should check it carefully every day and set your daily budget low. Most campaigns are not immediately profitable, and your first aim is to ensure you're breaking even, bearing in mind the long-term value of your new customers. As you make improvements to your click-through rate and cost per conversion, you'll find it takes less time to identify problems and opportunities and you develop a much better idea of what is likely to work for your business and its customers. However, you should never rely on intuition: always test.

CLICKS FOR FREE There's more to marketing than just getting your AdWords campaign working profitably. At the core is getting inside the conversation your customers are having inside their own heads. What are they thinking when they type their search phrase? What do they think when they see your ad? What do they do when they arrive at ➜

"The concept of 'build it and they will come' has no place in modern business. If you don't market your product or service effectively, it might as well not exist: no-one will ever know about it, much less buy it."

email, but make sure you've got it right before you enable that. Now click Create Report. Google will return you to the Report Center view, and after a few seconds your report will be completed. Click its name to view it.

Initially, you should order the report by Impressions, with the most at the top. Take a look at the "Cost/Conv" figure: do any numbers leap out at you as being either much lower than the others or, more worryingly, much higher? In our example (top right), compare lines 1 and 3. The conversion cost for line 3 is more than twice that

→ your landing page? What do they make of your product or service? You can answer these questions by regularly surveying your customers, especially in the early days, when you may well experience a forehead-slapping moment as you discover your customers don't see your product in the same way as you do, or they're not the customers you expected.

As far as possible, you should be open in your communication with customers. Make it easy for them to get in touch, even if this means exposing your support email on your website. If your product is an online service, install a support ticket system such as Hesk (www.hesk.com) so you don't end up playing email ping-pong. Questions that are regularly asked should either be added to your FAQ page or should result in changes to the site: remember, for every one visitor who bothers to ask a question there might be 20 who simply left your site unimpressed.

By developing an open dialogue with customers, you'll find they suggest improvements to your product or service. You need to work out if their ideas will actually improve your sales and profits, but new ideas are what push companies to continuing success.

Having a good product and proving there's a real person behind the website is the best way to garner priceless word-of-mouth recommendations. A Facebook user may have hundreds of "friends"; imagine the marketing potential of having them recommend you. As Mark Knopfler (almost) sang: "Money for nothing and your clicks for free".

FIVE STEPS TO SUCCESS I'd like to leave you with five tips that, in my view, differentiate successful businesses:

1 Do what you love, love what you do

If you've been following this book, you'll have picked a business based on your interests. It's much easier to devote the required mental and physical energy if you're naturally interested in what you sell. Setting up and running a business is challenging: you owe it to yourself, and the business, to choose a product or service that gets you excited.

Having said that, there are bound to be aspects of running a business that turn you on less than others. You have two options: either learn to love that task or outsource it. Take bookkeeping, for example. Few of us enjoy it, so you can either hire someone to take care of it or find a way of doing it that's (relatively) enjoyable. In my case, the online accounting service FreeAgent (www.freeagentcentral.com)

is so easy to use that I really don't mind doing my accounts, and I enjoy the control it gives me.

2 Never stop learning

Keep an open mind at all times, and don't assume you know anything without evidence to back it up. This applies to every aspect of the product development process as well as marketing, but also to the day-to-day running of the business.

Having started a business providing a service or product in a field you already had some expertise in, don't let that stop you improving. Nothing stands still, whether it's window cleaning, candle making or driving theory test services. Right now, on my desk, I have a book on Ajax (the increasingly popular group of web technologies) and another on Facebook application development. The first because it's a gap in my skills that needs fixing, and the second because it's a potential new platform for PassYourTheory to exploit.

I read books on marketing – most recently *Free* by Chris Anderson and *What Would Google Do?* by Jeff Jarvis – along with classic and contemporary fiction to "sharpen the saw". Any of these might inspire me; all will provoke me.

What can you do to improve your core skills beyond their current level? What can you do to bring those things that you are poor at up to an acceptable level?

3 Work on the business, not just in the business

This is the credo of the E-Myth series of books ("E" for "entrepreneur"). If you've started a business that plays to your technical strengths, the danger is that you'll end up spending all your time working on your product and doing administrative work, rather than working on making your business more successful.

Marketing and leadership are examples of the sorts of tasks that can easily get neglected in the excitement of cranking out the next great product, but without them your business has no chance of success.

Your reaction might be to protest that you started your own business specifically so that you could indulge your love of that particular business. Fine – just don't expect to make any money. It's a hard fact that you can't spend all your time playing with your toys. Learn to love marketing!

Of course, if you have the support of a partner or employees, you can farm out some of the aspects of running a business that you find less pleasant. But I don't recommend outsourcing marketing in the beginning: no-one knows your business like you do.

> **"Marketing and leadership can get neglected in the excitement of creating a product, but without them you have no chance of success."**

4 Always look on the bright side of life

Entrepreneurs are positive, "glass-is-half-full" individuals. Quite apart from the sheer amount of work required to bring a business into being and apply heart massage until it can breathe on its own, you'll also find yourself up against government bureaucracy and the inevitable naysayers.

How you deal with disaster is much more important than how you react in the good times. Captain Cock-up is the best instructor you could wish for, as long as you learn from it. Your business reflects *you*: if you're enthusiastic and confident, your business will seem that way to your customers, peers and suppliers.

A key element of this attitude is "never give up, never surrender". In short, don't let problems undermine your confidence in your own ability. Take comfort from the fact that all business owners mess up on a regular basis. If you can combine the willingness to learn with an unshakeable belief in your own ability, you'll stay confident without becoming arrogant – the ideal combination.

5 Work your nuts off

There's no getting away from it: setting up your own business is hard work. If it isn't, you're either unbelievably lucky or missing opportunities. While it's important to retain a sense of balance, there's no doubt that in the early days you'll be devoting much of your time to your business, whether you're setting up full-time or running it alongside your job.

Of all the qualities of the great entrepreneurs, a work ethic is shared by just about all of them. That's not to say hard work on its own guarantees success: effort expended without a plan is a waste of time. But without hard work, the greatest plan never sees the light of day.

BONUS TIP: GET A DOG See what I did there? Promised you five tips and then sneaked in a free bonus. "Get a dog"? I'm completely serious. If there's one action that has had more impact on my performance as a businessperson than any other, it's the regular walks Dizzy is subjected to. The size and breed of dog is unimportant (Dizzy is a Cairn terrier/Westie cross) as long as they like, or even demand, walks.

There are three reasons I recommend having a dog on the payroll. First, it makes you take exercise. If you work full-time for yourself, especially from home, the temptation is to sit at the computer all day pounding away at the keyboard without a break. This isn't good for you or your business. A brisk walk with the dog and you'll return refreshed and ready for the next challenge.

Second, running a business is a lonely activity. Even if you have a supportive family, friends and even

employees, being the boss is a lonely position. Having a dog sitting asleep in the corner of your office makes you feel less alone and lowers the blood pressure – and heaven knows running a business can often do the opposite.

Finally, by far the most important reason is this: the vast majority of good ideas I've had in the past few years have popped into my head as I've been walking the dog. It's essential not to listen to your MP3 player or to be distracted by anything else. Just start walking and either ponder a particular problem or think about nothing at all. Relaxing the analytical part of your brain allows the creative subconscious and right-brain to get your attention.

It is no exaggeration to say that Dizzy and her predecessor Ozzy have earned me many thousands of pounds from ideas that have dropped into my head during a walk. If you're a dog owner already, you probably don't need convincing. If not, why not borrow someone else's dog (with their permission, of course) and see what pops up?

And finally...

It's an exciting time to be starting a business, and doing so can be a life-changing experience. Work hard on generating a great product, build an effective platform and market your socks off and you have success in the palm of your hands. Good luck, and welcome to the club!

Daft as it may sound, a canine companion could make all the difference to your entrepreneurial career. Other domesticated animals are also available, but lack the crucial desire for walkies.

How to set up an online business

EDITORIAL

Editor
Kevin Partner

Managing Editor
Tim Danton   editor@pcpro.co.uk

Design and Layout
Adam Banks   adam@adambanks.com

Production
Bill Bagnall
Barry Collins
Steve Haines

LICENSING & SYNDICATION

International Licensing
Winnie Liesenfeld   020 7907 6314

Syndication
Jasmine Samra   020 7907 6132

ADVERTISING & MARKETING

Advertising Manager
Ben Topp   020 7907 6625

Digital Production Manager
Nicky Baker   020 7907 6056

MagBook Manager
Dharmesh Mistry   020 7907 6100

Marketing Manager
Claire Scrase   020 7907 6113

MANAGEMENT   020 7907 6000

Publishing Director
Ian Westwood

MD of Advertising
Julian Lloyd-Evans

Newstrade Director
Martin Belson

Chief Operating Officer
Brett Reynolds

Group Finance Director
Ian Leggett

Chief Executive
James Tye

Chairman
Felix Dennis

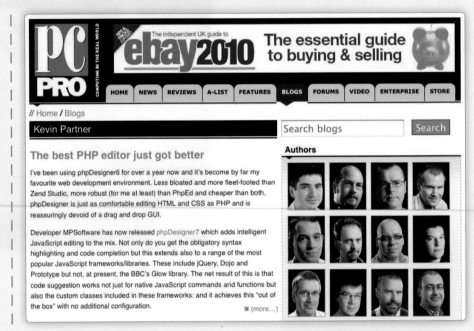

You've read the book – now read the blog. Catch up with Kevin Partner's latest tips for internet businesses, along with opinions and reviews from his PC Pro colleagues, at www.pcpro.co.uk/blogs/category/online-business

ISBN 1-906372-31-4